HOPE
AND
HELP
FOR THE
ADDICTED

HOPE
AND
HELP
FOR THE
ADDICTED

Jeff VanVonderen

SPIRE

© 1991, 2004 by Jeff VanVonderen

Published by Revell
a division of Baker Publishing Group
P.O. Box 6287, Grand Rapids, MI 49516-6287
www.revellbooks.com

Spire edition published 2011
ISBN 978-0-8007-8815-5

Previously published by Bethany House in 1995 as *Good News for the Chemically Dependent and Those Who Love Them*

Printed in the United States of America

11   12   13   14   15   16   17   7   6   5   4   3   2   1

To my father, Wayne VanVonderen, who taught me that it is okay to make waves. Special thanks to my family and the friends who have stood by me through difficult times.

Contents

PART **1**

DARKENED IN UNDERSTANDING, ALIENATED FROM LIFE

Introduction

I raised my kids in the '80s and '90s. Like many other parents, I was concerned about ways to help them stay out of trouble with drugs and alcohol. During the first presidential term of her husband, Ronald, Nancy Reagan announced her "Just Say No" campaign, an approach that was championed in the public schools by a program called DARE (Drug Abuse Resistance Education). I was encouraged that the problem was getting such aggressive and widespread attention. But a little less than two decades after Nancy Reagan rolled out "Just Say No," the news was bleak. On February 15, 2001, *Time Magazine* published the bad news:

> Here's a news flash: "Just Say No" is not an effective anti-drug message. And concerning DARE, "The findings were grim: 20-year-olds who'd had DARE classes were no less likely to have smoked marijuana or cigarettes, drunk alcohol, used 'illicit' drugs like cocaine or heroin, or caved in to peer pressure than kids who'd never been exposed to DARE," referring to study published in August 1999 volume of *The Journal of Consulting and Clinical Psychology.*

And did you know that the federal government spent over $19 billion on the "war on drugs" in 2003, with more than another $20 billion spent on the state level? Chances are, though, if you are reading this, you don't need statistics to convince you that drug and alcohol prevention efforts have not been ineffective.

This is a book for people who *did not say no*, and the family members and friends who love them. And there is good news contained within for all. If you are a family member or friend, you will find principles that will enable you to experience health and fullness in the midst of your painful times of crisis. You will also learn to understand the unhealthy ways in which you may be reacting to the dependency of your loved one. And anyone who is concerned about healthy families will discover relationship concepts that will be instrumental in preventing harmful dependencies in loved ones.

You see, chemical dependency does not occur in a vacuum. It is a relational issue. The quality of relationships between the chemically dependent person and other persons in families, in churches, at work, and in society is profoundly damaged. The odds are great that, if ignored, generations of loved ones will feel the crippling effects of someone's harmful dependency.

For an addict, living with an active addiction is like living on a tightrope. And living with—or even loving—that person is like looking up and watching them as they try to keep up the balancing act. It's a rather daunting experience because they aren't a tightrope walker, they are just your loved one. Plus, they are under the influence, which makes them even worse at tightrope walking. In addition to feeling like you need to watch the tightrope act continuously, at times it's actually as if you can't help yourself. All kinds of other things demand and deserve your attention as well—other family members, jobs, hobbies, church, etc. And yet even while you are trying to attend to all the other life concerns around you, you're always thinking, wondering, worrying about the person on the tightrope. So the person's problems and their consequences invade and permeate every area of your life.

And then they slip and fall, or they almost fall, or they look like they're going to fall. That's the latest crisis, phone call, outburst, the latest broken promise. But somehow they always manage to hook the rope with a fingernail and drag themselves back up to continue the "show." Or, because those who love them don't want them to plunge to their deaths, they push them back up by giving them help that just keeps them living on the tightrope, where everyone wishes they weren't living in the first place. And so the cycle goes on and on.

Think about it. How often have you tried, with the best of intentions, to help yourself or your loved one through a problem or crisis, only to discover that the help is not helpful, or has even contributed to the problem? And one day you realize that you have been supporting and helping to prolong on the outside the very thing you do not support on the inside.

But it doesn't have to be that way. Things can change.

Individuals and families become dysfunctional by accident. But they get well on purpose, and this book will help you begin to do exactly that. Part 1 will do this by exposing the nature and process of dependency, codependency, and shame. Part 2 explains how to help those who are unhappy with the effects of their own or someone else's problem with mood-altering substances.

Be encouraged. Help is on the way.

1

The Road to Addiction Is Ugly, Not Scenic

I have a friend named Dan Adler who is the minister of music at Church of the Open Door in Minneapolis. He's a man with a heart for the tired and broken of the world. In his song that follows, "Image of the Maker," Dan paints a picture of the human struggle in a way that I think is intricately related to the issue of addiction.

> There's an empty place in every man,
> And though he may not understand,
> He spends a lifetime tryin' to satisfy
> The need inside that he cannot hide.
> Some people seek prosperity
> But it leaves you wantin' more, you see.
> You can buy all of the things money can buy,
> And though you try, it won't satisfy.
>
> There's a missing piece in our puzzled souls
> That leaves us feelin' we're unwhole.
> As we try to fit our own piece in,
> We can't begin to fit it in.

Some people try to get away,
But they find that they are here to stay.
Some search for love, some search for fame,
But in the end they feel the same.

'Cause the Image of the Maker was stamped on our
  hearts,
But our wickedness tore our relationship apart,
And left us with a yearning within
That won't be satisfied until we're joined
With our Maker again.[1]

Symptom of Need

One-fourth of those surveyed in a 1978 Gallup poll admitted that alcohol use had negatively affected their family life. One out of four! At the same time, only 8 percent of all surveyed said they would turn for help to the church or its trained personnel if they or a family member had a drinking problem.

In churches where drinking is approached very conservatively (as a sin), half as many people drink as in those that hold a more liberal view (a matter of personal choice). Yet in the conservative churches, of those who choose to drink anyway, twice as many develop alcohol-related problems. That means that the number of problem drinkers is the same in both kinds of churches.

Chemical dependency is a problem that has reached epidemic proportions in our society. There is no typical alcohol or chemically dependent person. If it had the power to choose whom it would affect, chemical dependency would not be very good at distinguishing between the rich or poor, young or old, black or white, male or female, white- or blue-collar worker.

1. Dan Adler, "Image of the Maker," copyright 1984.

Holding a religious view that prohibits alcohol use proves no more effective in the area of preventing chemical-related problems than holding a liberal view. Moving from New Jersey to Arizona serves no purpose in overcoming the problem once it is present. Why not? Because alcohol and drugs are not the cause, only a symptom of what runs much deeper.

Confronting the Wrong Cause?

In Mark 7:15, Jesus said, "There is nothing that enters a man from outside which can defile him." If Jesus is right in this passage, why are so many families and churches characterized by a "barriers" approach to preventing "defilement"? That is, telling people how bad it is for them to drink this, eat that, or go there, making a rule against it, and then trying to make them good rule-followers. This represents such an inadequate view of health. Just because a person avoids or stops using chemicals and goes out for football or band does not mean he or she is a healthy person. Attendance at church instead of the local bar is not the same as health either. Yet so much of the effort put forth in families and churches is toward extinguishing one behavior and rewarding another.

Jesus' statement confronts all of our efforts to solve or prevent problems by avoiding something that does not have the power to cause the problem in the first place. What a waste of time! This approach urges us to define health in terms of outside behavior instead of inside fullness. It provides no help or support once a person has broken through the barrier. It simply does not address the cause of the problem.

So what is the cause? Environment? Neighborhood, peers, opportunities or lack of opportunity, and other external factors do play upon a person's life. However, these are not the cause. Poor choices? People's poor choices contribute to their problems and leave them with consequences to untangle. So does the lack of healthy past and present relationships. Shame contributes, as does ignorance, self-righteousness, dishonesty, and denial. Later in the book I will address in more specific ways the role these factors have in the process of addiction. But while these play a profound part, they are not the cause either.

The Cause

So what is the cause? It is *seeking life from idols*. At first glance, my answer to that question might seem so "religious" as to be of no use at all. This is hardly the case. The truth is that this concept, which we have too long seen as purely theological, has many very practical ramifications in our lives. I believe that at the heart of all harmful dependencies is the issue of idolatry. A grasp of this concept is essential as a foundation for understanding the processes of chemical dependency and codependency, or, for that matter, any unhealthy dependencies. Let me explain idolatry.

Remember the account of the Garden of Eden in the book of Genesis? It tells of God's creation of Adam and Eve. God was their source and sustainer. He placed them in relationships (with Himself and each other) and in an environment in which all of their needs were met. This is much of what I believe God meant when He said, "This is very good." There was a tree in the garden that was off-limits. Genesis 2:17 says, "For in the day that you eat of it you shall surely die." They ate and they died.

There have been volumes of books written and thousands of sermons preached about what mankind acquired when Adam and Eve ate from the tree: a sinful nature, fallen perceptions, depraved desires. What did man get when he disobeyed God? "You shall surely die," warned God. And it was so. But getting

18

death is not getting anything; it is losing something. Man *lost* life in the Garden of Eden.

Understanding death and life is not really so difficult. It is like darkness and light. Darkness is not the opposite of light; it is the absence of light. The way to be in the light is not by trying hard not to be in the dark. It is by coming into or turning on a light. Death is not the opposite of life; it is the absence of life. The way to have life is not by trying hard not to be dead. It is by coming to what can give life.

God's Solution to Death

"I have come that they may have *life*" (John 10:10); "I am the bread of *life*" (John 6:48); "I am the resurrection and the *life*" (John 11:25); and "I am the way, the truth, and the *life*" (John 14:6). Why did Jesus come offering life? Because we did not have it. Romans 5:12 says that "death spread to all men, because all sinned." To argue whether we are dead because Adam sinned or because we sin misses the point. The point is that we lack life.

You will notice in the Bible that there were many people who were aware of their lack of life. Lepers and tax collectors, blind and lame, sick and poor—these are the ones to whom Jesus had a healing, life-giving ministry. He was the life, and they knew they lacked it. Pharisees, on the other hand, were oblivious to their lack of life because of their religious activities and flawless theology. The rich were unaware of their lack because of their great wealth, politicians because of their power and influence. Jesus had little, if any, ministry to them.

What does the Garden of Eden and understanding life and death have to do with idolatry, or chemical dependency? Plenty! Ever since man lost life, he has tried to regain it by turning to two inadequate sources: things and self-effort.

But God is the only true source of life, value, and meaning. Therefore, no amount of things or effort can ever produce the desired result.

Anything besides God to which we turn, positive or negative, in order to find life, value, and meaning is idolatry: money, property, jewels, sex, clothes, church buildings, educational degrees, anything! Because of Christ's performance on the cross, life, value, and purpose are available to us in gift form only. Anything we do, positive or negative, to earn that which is life by our own performance is idolatrous: robbing a bank, cheating on our spouse, people-pleasing, swindling our employer, attending church, giving 10 percent, playing the organ for twenty years, anything!

Idolatry: A Matter of "Why"

Is money bad? No. Is having money bad? Again, the answer is no. At its core, idolatry is not about *what*, but about *why*. Why does a person earn or have money? The answer to that question is what determines if money is an idol. If a person sees money as having the power to cause him to have value and security, then that person has an idolatrous relationship with money. He will continually pursue more money.

Let's say George lacks money. To him this might mean that he is an inadequate, defective person. He might also believe that having money will prove him adequate, give him a sense of being capable, and earn the respect of self and others. George sets out on a course to earn and acquire money. He sets a goal that, when reached, will tell him and everyone else that he is OK.

Because he is convinced that money on the outside can bring fullness on the inside, he might be willing to pay some prices in other areas of his life to continue his pursuit. He may work long hours and neglect his family. He may cheat on his taxes, swindle his company, keep extra change at the grocery store, or bet on the horses. He might give a lot of money to the church so that God will give him even more in return.

The truth is, however, that money does not have the power to do for him what George expects. If money were able to make George OK, he could reach his goal, be OK, and stop pursuing money. But George is turning to an inadequate source. He might reach his goal, but until George realizes the impotence of money, he will never be free to stop pursuing it.

In addition, the longer George pursues money, the harder it will be to stop. He has too many past efforts to justify. More than likely, his headlong quest has damaged his relationship with family members. He has tried to justify this with presents and with the promise that it will be worth it down the road. He may have sacrificed his integrity in his dealings with others. The IRS might be very interested in his bookkeeping and tax records. George must continue to invest time, energy, and emotion in an effort to rescue what he has already invested. If this process continues, he might end up with a lot of money and nothing else.

All Roads (but One) Lead to Addiction

The constant gnawing in the pit of his stomach might force George to consider a couple of alternatives. First, he can admit that money is inadequate and that he has wasted his time, family, and health for nothing. He might become depressed. He might medicate himself into oblivion. Some people commit suicide at this point. Others invest all of their money in real estate, thinking that *it* will provide what money could not. Some find life, value, and meaning as a gift through a relationship with Christ.

Second, he can decide that he has not tried hard enough and invest more time, energy, and emotion than before. The fact that he continues to pursue money without attention paid to the prices incurred demonstrates that George is addicted to money.

Addiction is the ultimate end of idolatry. In 1 Corinthians 6:12, Paul said, "All things are lawful for me, but all things are not helpful. All things are lawful for me, but I will not be brought under the power of any." We have just walked through the process of George's being brought under the power of a lawful thing. Money, which in a relationship with Christ would be a gift to serve him, has become George's master, being served at all costs.

Understanding Terms

Chapters 2–6 are a description of chemical dependency and its ramifications. They are about individuals and families brought under the power of chemicals. The time has come to cut through all of the smoke that clouds this issue and to begin to understand what we are really facing in our families and churches.

Before proceeding to those chapters, I wish to explain certain words and concepts to undergird our further study of the dependencies related to chemical use. The word *chemical* in the phrase "chemical dependency" refers to alcohol and all other mood-altering drugs. The word refers to any substance that changes the mood or alters the emotions of the user. I have chosen to describe the spectrum of mood-altering drugs in five categories: depressants, stimulants, hallucinogens, narcotics, and over-the-counter drugs that can easily be abused. This is meant to be only a sample.

Depressants

Main types: alcohol, sedatives (sleeping pills), tranquilizers (Valium), and barbiturates (downers).

Psychological effects: poor judgment; inability to concentrate; distorted perceptions; incoherence; aggressive behavior; affects entire central nervous system.

Physical effects: drowsiness; slurred speech; lack of coordination; lack of energy; sleep; coma; restlessness, anxiety, cramps, and vomiting during withdrawal.

Stimulants

Main types: cocaine, amphetamines, caffeine.

Psychological effects: high; increase in self-confidence, sexual desire, sociability, and energy; diminished sense of tiredness; depression during withdrawal.

Physical effects: elevated blood pressure and heart rate; perspiration; increased tolerance to presence of drugs.

Hallucinogens

Main types: LSD, marijuana, PCP (angel dust), mescaline.

Psychological effects: hallucinations, changes in perceptions, sense of being detached from one's own body, panic, lowering of inhibitions.

Physical effects: varied.

Narcotics

Main types: opium, morphine, heroin, codeine.

Psychological effects: relief of emotional consequences of pain, euphoria.

Physical effects: acts on particular opiate receptors; physically and emotionally painful withdrawal; cramps; sweating; panic; chills.

Over-the-Counter Drugs

Main types: OTC stimulants (caffeine, chocolate, nicotine), sleep aids (effects similar to sedatives), pain killers (aspirin, acetaminophen, ibuprophen), cold remedies (Contac, Dristan, and those containing alcohol), weight-control products (Dexatrim).

Psychological effects: emotional or psychological dependency on drugs' effects.

Physical effects: intoxication; hyperactivity; nervousness; physical dependency on the drugs' effects.[2]

A further word on alcohol. Alcohol is a drug. It is the most abused, most deadly, and most underestimated of all the chemicals used in our society. To feel the weight of this last statement, consider this: Imagine that a 747 airliner full of passengers crashed every week and everyone aboard died. That is how many people die weekly in alcohol-related traffic accidents. Sixty percent of all violent crimes are alcohol-related. If alcohol was discovered in a laboratory today, it would be classified as a controlled substance, which means that it would only be available via a doctor's prescription. Despite all of this, alcohol use is legal and socially accepted. In many cases, it is socially *expected*. I don't share, even in the slightest way, the sense of relief expressed to me by many parents who say, "It's no big deal, my son/daughter only drinks."

Defining *dependency* is a little more difficult. To say "I depend upon you," for instance (*depend* being a verb), means that I rely on you; I believe in you; I'm counting on you; you are the object of my trust. But it is possible, while I am depending upon you, to depend in varying degrees on others as well:

2. For an excellent glossary of terms related to the use of mood-altering drugs, see page 200 of Jay Strack's book, *Drugs and Drinking* (Nashville: Thomas Nelson, 1985).

myself, parents, spouse, job, religion, public opinion, even Jesus Christ. These are not necessarily mutually exclusive.

Dependency, a noun, means "the state of being dependent." Jesus does not want me to be dependent upon Him as well as you, my parents, spouse, job, goods, or religion as my source of life and value. He wants me to be dependent upon Him alone. Because He is the only adequate source of these things, He provides resources to meet my needs. You might call it "God dependency"—the state that results from the process of choosing to depend upon Him more and more. Chemical *dependency*, on the other hand, is the *state* that results from the process of increasingly depending (verb) on chemical use to meet life needs. Chemical dependency fails to meet those needs and isolates people from other resources.

There are also the phenomena of *physical* and *psychological/emotional addiction*. Physical addiction occurs when the cells of the body change the way they function because of the frequent use of certain chemical substances. The cells become accustomed to the presence of those substances. Physical addiction to nicotine is what causes a craving in the person who is trying to quit smoking cigarettes. Addiction to caffeine is why you have a headache if you don't get coffee soon enough. Addiction to sugar causes that nagging itch when you don't get your daily dessert.

Psycho-emotional addiction can be present without physical addiction. It is the result of using chemicals to solve problems or meet emotional needs instead of turning to God-given relationships and resources. If we turn to families and the body of Christ and they function as God intended, we are supported, our needs are met, and the need for chemical use seems ludicrous. However, if we turn to these resources and they do not do what God intended, or if we turn long enough to chemicals instead to meet our psycho-emotional needs, we will eventually lose our relationships. Then the need for further chemical use is reinforced.

Abuse is any use of a chemical substance that causes the user to become or act in a way that is other than normal for him. If a person with a mellow temperament becomes mean after using, that is abuse. If a person is normally cranky and uses a chemical to become pleasant, that is abuse. I cannot count the number of times I have heard people say that after they (or their dad, mom, friend) have a few drinks, they can really be themselves. They are abusing chemicals.

I might stay up until 3:00 a.m. and get only four hours of sleep. If I can drink a couple of cups of coffee before work and a couple more when I get there so I will not feel or act as tired as I really am, that is abuse. I might come home from a terrible day at work, frustrated about my job and tense with my boss. If I have a drink "just to unwind," that is abuse. Chemical manipulation of feelings is not healthy and damages relationships. In healthy relationships, the manipulation is not necessary.

Emotions are an instantaneous internal response to the world and are not premeditated. Talking about emotions in terms of good and bad, right and wrong, positive and negative feelings, communicates morality. But the capacity to feel emotions is part of what it means to be created in the image of God. He feels things; we feel things. It is part of being human. Emotions are not right or wrong; they just are. Any behavior that results or attitude that develops as a person responds to internal emotions involves a choice on his part. Therefore, actions and attitudes do have moral implications. This is why it is so important for us to know how we feel.

Let me explain. Feelings are like telegrams that give us a message about our relationship with someone or something outside ourselves. They are there to get us to learn something about that relationship. We can choose to use them as a bridge or barrier. If we choose to ignore the signal, we waste an opportunity to grow. On the other hand, an emotion might tell us that we need to make some different choices in that relationship.

Even anger (which Jesus felt and we are told to feel in Eph. 4:26) can serve as a bridge in our relationship with the person with whom we feel angry. However, to use anger as a bridge, we have to act in a moral way that builds the relationship. That way is described in Ephesians 4:25: "Therefore, putting away lying, each one speak truth with his neighbor, for we are members of one another." To act in a way that tears down, such as blowing up that person's car, is immoral and inappropriate. If we ignore or nurse anger (let the "sun go down on" our wrath, see Eph. 4:26), the devil gets an opportunity to use our anger and affect our actions at a future date. Pretending you do not feel anger once you do will not eliminate angry feelings. Settle the situation. Do not be controlled by your emotions, but do not ignore or try to control them either. Feel them. They will teach you about what is important to you. Recognize your feelings and use them to make appropriate, relationship-building choices.

Needs, if met, allow us to function as productive members of our various systems: family, church, school, work, peers. As human beings we have numerous physiological needs—food, shelter, clothing, and so forth. Although these needs are vital to life, I wish to discuss spiritual, emotional, and psychological needs because chemical dependency has much sooner identifiable consequences in these areas.

Through counseling others, gaining understanding into the gospel, and learning about myself, I have come to see three basic needs in human beings. Before I list them, let me declare that the Bible tells how God has already acted to meet those needs before we are even aware of them. First, we need to be convinced that we are loved and accepted without conditions. We do not have to perform, do tricks, be polite, act crazy, be cute, or quote Bible verses. When we make a mistake, love and acceptance are not withdrawn. Love is based upon the fullness of the one giving it and not upon the performance of the one receiving it. Earned love does not build us because it is not about us, it is about our behavior.

Second, we need to be convinced that we are important, worthwhile, capable, and special. Biblical terms that communicate the same concepts are *gifted*, *chosen*, *needed*, and *created for a purpose*. This message must be unconditional also, not withdrawn for lack of performance.

Third, we need to be convinced that we are not alone when we face life's problems. Others have the same feelings and problems as we do and stand behind us in our struggle. And again, the presence and support of others must be unconditional.

Some people are convinced of these things. You know who they are. Some are not convinced of these things at all. You know who they are too. Let me make three assertions at this point. First, the major purpose of the family and the body of Christ is to convince their members that they are loved and accepted, they are capable and special, and they do not face life alone. But isn't that just the message of the gospel? God loves you and accepts you. He chooses you, frees you, forgives you, creates you anew, has gifted you, has caused you to be His friend and heir, invites you into His presence; and you are not alone.

Second, the degree to which people are convinced of these things is the degree to which they are able to and will love, accept, serve, and give to others, and exercise their spiritual gifts out of freedom and fullness. Empty people can only counterfeit obedience and service, and do that out of duty, obligation, guilt, or trying to repay God (which is not possible).

Third, in an unconditional environment, where love and acceptance confirm value bought by Christ, mistakes and problems are learning opportunities. Granted, unconditional relationships are rare. But we must aggressively seek them out in order to be reminded of our settled acceptance and value based on God's grace toward us in Jesus. Being supported unconditionally enables people to continue a recovery based on honesty and vulnerability.

The story is different, however, in a conditional environment where self-effort earns value. Mistakes are opportunities to feel bad about yourself, to try harder to be perfect (which is not possible), and to pretend that problems do not exist. In this environment, people tend to become isolated from the help and support they need to overcome problems. In addition, in their efforts to earn acceptance and love, they lose their integrity and eventually their recovery.

A Useless Debate

"Do you think alcoholism (or chemical dependency) is a *sin* or a *sickness*?" is a question I am asked every time I present a seminar. There is a great debate between members of the religious community and professionals in the field of chemical dependency as to whether chemical dependency is a sin or a disease. I do not intend to spend much time debating someone else's or defending my own point of view on this issue. This book will be of value to individuals and families who are in the clutches of a chemical problem, no matter on which side of the debate they stand.

I will present my approach as a counselor, however, because it represents for families and individuals an integration of the practical good news of recovery from chemical dependency with the theological good news of Christ's gift and who we are because of it. My approach is the result of extensive experience and training in chemical dependency and study of Scripture. It is not the only approach, but it is mine.

I believe that chemical dependency is a disease. Drinking is not a disease. Being drunk is not a disease. Nevertheless, the state of being dependent upon chemicals to the exclusion of healthy relationships with other resources *is* a disease.

The Greek word for sin, *hamartia*, literally means "missing the mark." Does chemical dependency miss God's mark for chemical use? Yes. Therefore, it can be said that chemical dependency is a sin. But, while calling chemical dependency a moral issue is correct, it is also simplistic. Ultimately everything may be called a moral issue. Calling the chemically dependent person a sinner (someone who misses the mark) is certainly a correct diagnosis, yet it is inadequate to motivate repentance because of the presence of the disease itself. The chemically dependent person is an individual who not only has substituted chemicals for helpful resources as the source of life-needs, but who has also developed a mind-set that convinces him that he is fine. Everyone (you, me, his boss, his parents, the president of the United States) and everything else is the problem. This false belief is called *delusion*, and it will be discussed at length in chapter 2. Delusion is what keeps people from seeing the truth.

Some persons feel that calling chemical dependency a disease is letting the dependent person off the hook. Actually, the opposite is true. The revelation that you have a disease makes you responsible to do something about it. Only a fool would do nothing once he found out he had cancer or diabetes. And only someone who is deluded would neglect getting help once he realized he was chemically dependent. Having cancer is not a sin. Abusing your body (with cigarettes, for instance) in a way that causes cancer *is* a sin. However, once cancer is present, to simply quit smoking is not enough. A disease is present that needs to be treated so life and relationships can be resumed.

With chemical dependency, to quit using chemicals is not enough to effect a cure. Nor is it enough to get the person to feel bad about himself because of his behavior so that he will change. As a matter of fact, when the person felt bad in the past, he turned to chemical use. A disease now exists that needs to be treated so life and relationships can be resumed. In addition to giving up his inadequate chemical resources, the person needs to learn to rely upon new, adequate resources—Jesus, family, the body of Christ, and healthy relationship skills. He also needs to reconsider his view of himself and his world, both of which have been greatly distorted.

Additional comparisons can be made between chemical dependency and other diseases. Chemical dependency is describable and predictable. The medical term for this is *pathology*. Everyone being affected by chemical dependency who reads this book will be able to see himself because chemical dependency is a disease that looks basically the same in everyone affected. A process appears in all those affected. There may be a difference in the rate at which individuals and families are affected, but for everyone, the dependency gets worse if neglected. If recognized and treated, people improve as with other diseases. If left untreated, chemical dependency leads to the death of relationships and eventually to the insanity and/or death of the dependent person.

Again, this is the approach that I use. I think it is a waste of time trying to convince persons of the cause (sin) of something they do not even know they have. Rather, I choose to approach chemically dependent individuals by describing to them what I see and leading them to make decisions concerning what to do about it.

Finally, families are *systems*, just like societies or the body of Christ. Members of a system are interdependent. You may have a family member who acts as if he is independent, but in reality he is very dependent upon other family members in many ways. Not only that, but everything that a family member does, feels, or experiences affects the other members of the system, in subtle or obvious ways. Chemical dependency is a problem that has devastating effects upon the chemical user. But that is not all—family members, friends, and fellow church members are affected because they are part of a system with the dependent person.

The next several chapters are about the dynamics of dependency and codependency and their frightening effects on individuals and families.

2

Futility of Mind

Imagine that you have just arrived at your church building to begin attending a seminar, which consists of a series of four or five sessions concerning alcohol and drug problems and how they affect people. You sit in the same general area, perhaps in the same seat as you do each Sunday. Your head is filled with various thoughts. *Why did Pastor bring a speaker in to talk about this? This isn't a problem here! . . . I hope no one thinks I'm here for me or my family! . . . I don't know why I bothered coming. This isn't going to help any more than anything else has. . . . I wish Frank and Louise were here. This might help them stop their son from being such a bad influence on my daughter.*

Why People Use Chemicals

Whenever I present a "Good News for the Chemically Dependent" seminar, I begin with the question, "Why do people use chemicals?" The purpose of the question is to unearth any and all helpful and harmful attitudes toward chemical use and chemical users. Many times people are reluctant to answer. In church gatherings especially, people are often afraid that answering the question might arouse the suspicion of those around them. When people do not answer, we wait quietly for an amount of time that seems appropriate.

When the silence seems too lengthy, I ask, "How many of you don't know *anyone* who uses one chemical substance or another?" Invariably, almost no one raises his hand, which means that *everyone* knows someone who uses alcohol or drugs. I then ask, "If you were to ask that person why he uses it, what would be his answer?" By giving audience members permission to give someone else's answer, I have freed them to give their own answer to the very first question concerning why people use chemicals! I am distressed to see, firsthand, the pressure people feel in some churches *not* to be transparent.

Some people say, "If I were to ask the person about whom I'm thinking, he would say, 'Get off my back, it's none of your business!'" But many people begin to respond with reasons for which they or others use chemicals: to relax, to escape, to relieve stress, for medicinal purposes, peer pressure, lack of spirituality, sin, for fun, moral weakness, and to socialize. Very few people in church settings answer, "To get high." It is as if church people are not supposed to know that.

Use this opportune time to compare your answer to this list or to add any of your own that are missing. Have you thought of any additional reasons?

Let's now leave the seminar setting and use the rest of this chapter to discuss the accuracy or inaccuracy of these theories.

Deciding to Start

I have come to the view that there are actually just two reasons why people use chemicals. Initially, the first reason might sound simplistic. People use chemicals simply because they *decide to*; it is their choice. As you read additional chapters, you will come to understand that this view is very helpful because it makes chemical use an issue of personal choice and responsibility. If I am choosing to use, then I can choose not to. All of the reasons given are not really reasons at all, but are simply factors or even needs, most of which are present in the lives of everyone at one time or another.

Everyone needs ways to relieve the stress that is so common in our high-speed, success-oriented culture. Everyone is a sinner. Everyone has the need to relax, to unwind, to have fun, and even to escape. Even *Jesus* needed to escape! Remember John the Baptist, Jesus' cousin, the one who baptized Him, the one who was the forerunner? In Matthew 14, John has just been beheaded. How does Jesus feel? The text does not say. But we may be able to discover some things from the way in which Jesus reacted upon being told of John's death. Verse 13 says, "When Jesus heard it, He departed from there by boat to a deserted place by Himself."

When I was in seminary, my best friend was killed in a car accident by a drunk driver. My parents were visiting my wife and me at the time, and we were all scrunched together in our little one-bedroom apartment. I received a telephone call in the middle of the afternoon with the news of the accident. When I first found out, I did not want to be with anyone, not Holly, not my parents, not anyone! I felt angry, hurt, numb, confused. My friend had loved Jesus with a tremendous love. He approached his ministry to church youth and his job as a public school teacher with a vitality that attested to the power of God. His death did not make sense. I had to escape, to be alone. I had to confront God with "Why?"

Jesus had just managed to find a lonely spot when five thousand people interrupted His solitude. Not only that, but they had forgotten their lunches! He met their needs. But He still had needs too.

Immediately Jesus made His disciples get into the boat and go before Him to the other side, while He sent the multitudes away. And when He had sent the multitudes away, He went up on a mountain by Himself to pray. And when evening had come, He was alone there. (Matt. 14:22–23)

The text is not explicit about this, but it almost seems as if Jesus was not finished sorting out His questions and feelings. Nevertheless, people choose to escape at times. Some escapes build people, while others tear them down.

Selling Promises

We all have peer pressure, not just teenagers. We all feel the need to fit in (to not be alone). In fact, the reason why advertising campaigns work is due to the magnitude of this need. Advertisements are not as much about the product as they are about a promise made concerning the benefits of possessing the product. Billboards, television commercials, and magazine ads insinuate that we are not quite OK the way we are. However, *if* we had this pair of jeans with a certain insignia on the rump, that pair of sneakers with the certain symbol on the side, or the other brand of liquor with the power to surround us with friends, *then* we would be OK.

Notice that you will never see an overweight person making a commercial for the latest designer jeans. You will never see a person make a cigarette ad from a hospital bed.

I used a certain shampoo because I needed my hair to be "bouncin' and behavin.'" You will see from my picture that it really worked too, but what are the chances that I will ever be asked to do a television spot for that shampoo? The fact is, advertising people know that you cannot sell products that will cause the buyers to identify themselves with people who are overweight, sick, or bald. So they present the promise that certain material objects have the power to meet our need to fit in. If we believe the promise, we will buy the product. It's as simple as that.

These illustrations point out that everyone experiences the needs or drives that are on the "reason list" at the beginning of this chapter. But *not* everyone chooses to use chemicals to fulfill them. Some people choose healthy ways to deal with stress, such as jogging, taking a vacation, or practicing the serenity prayer. Some choose to use chemicals to escape the stress. Others choose suicide as the solution to their stressful situation. Some decide to use chemicals to have fun, or as a means to fit in (or at least to numb the pain of feeling like they do not belong). Other people choose other alternatives to meet these needs.

Thinking about a chemical user as if he were using for a reason places the responsibility of the use on the reason and not on the user. What if negative consequences begin to appear because of the use? The user is really somewhat of a victim at this point because the reasons are still present. But what if a person uses because he decides to use, and it causes negative consequences? Are relationships being affected in negative ways? Does he have to break the law to use? Is he spending money for alcohol that could be used in better ways? At that point he can decide not to use, thereby eliminating the negative consequences. The first reason people use chemicals, then, is because they decide to; it is their choice.

Unable to Stop

However, now things become more complicated. The second reason why people use chemicals is because they *can't decide not to*. More accurately, they can decide not to use, but they no longer have the resources or abilities to be able to follow through with their decision. While this seems to rationalize the person's use, it is really a description of the state of not being able to *will* one's self out of certain behavior patterns and into others. Paul described this state in Romans 7:15 and 19:

> For what I am doing, I do not understand. For what I *will* to do, that I do not practice; but what I hate, that I do. For the good that I *will* to do, I do not do; but the evil I *will* not to do, that I practice (italics mine).

Persons who have never experienced alcohol or drug addiction may not be able to understand. An easier-to-understand addiction would be food or uncontrollable eating habits. For example, someone who is on a diet accepts a dinner invitation. Upon arriving, he discovers that his host is serving his favorite pie. All of a sudden, he gives himself a dozen "good reasons" why he can go off his diet (this one time). He explains to his family how he has starved himself extra hard just so he could have this one piece of pie. "It's all right," he says. "I'll go back on my diet tomorrow." The tendency to back off from commitments and rationalize is a signal that an addiction is present.

Promising to play with the kids while continuing to watch the football game instead is the same kind of phenomenon. This experience occurs in the lives of many television viewers, as well as video game buffs, gamblers, corporate types, and others who act compulsively, pay prices, and rationalize away the cost.

Being a Christian does not exempt us from these struggles. Feeling bad enough, praying hard, or having the right theology will not eliminate the problem. Gathering the resources and relationships necessary to become an individual who acts consistently with decisions to quit one thing or to follow through with another is the first step. Needs must be met and the pain that chemicals, food, television, video games, sex, or gambling help us avoid must be healed.

As a matter of fact, if a relationship with Christ does not drive us *into* the events that have caused us pain in order to face them, but instead serves as an escape that enables us to avoid problem relationships, then it has become as much of an escape to unreality as chemicals. Jesus did not come so we could "get high on Jesus." He did not come to end our problems, make us rich, or numb our pain. He came to blaze a trail *through* pain. He invites us to follow, secure in the knowledge that we have Him, His Spirit, and hopefully His body and our families for support to face our pain.

A Brief Personal History

My college career consisted of attending four colleges in five years. There was also a two-month hitch in the Army in the middle of that time. Immediately after high school, I attended a private college where I began to use alcohol and drugs quite regularly. I am still amazed to think of the incredibly short period of time it took for me to get heavily involved with chemicals. My grade point average dropped from almost a 3.5 in high school to a 2.5 my first semester in college. Second semester it was 1.5. I was placed on probation. I had made the freshman basketball team but then quit. I told everyone the reason I quit was because the coach was a jerk. The real reason was because I could not both play basketball and use drugs as much as I wanted. I made my choice. Never having learned to be responsible for myself and my choices meant I had to find someone to blame. I observed that the college was for "rich kids" and did not really understand my unique needs. I decided that the college really did not know how to educate people properly.

Since, to me, the college was obviously the problem, I transferred to another. The next college happened to be one that was academically less difficult, just by coincidence of course. I continued to use during that time, blame *this* college, and lie to my family (who was paying the price for me to party). My grade point average went up, which in my mind proved the ineffectiveness of the first college. However, if I had been at the previous college, or if I had been evaluated on my actual learning, my grade point would have been lower. I cheated on tests and assignments to balance the effects my chemical use was having on my grades. I justified this by saying, "Everyone is doing it, and the teachers don't care anyway." I lasted there one semester.

About this time, my folks began to catch on to my act. They were not aware of the extent of my chemical use, but they knew I was being very irresponsible. While they still tended to believe my excuses (I think they needed to), they threatened to cut off my college funds if I did not start getting better grades. My response to their threats was to blame the school, blame them for pressuring me to perform, and enlist in the Army. *That way,* I thought, *I can get the GI bill and party on the Army's tab.* My parents could not threaten me anymore, either.

Well, I could not get as high in the Army as I wanted (and at that point needed) to. The only chemicals I could get were 3.2 beer from the commissary and codeine when I was able to fake a bad enough cold. I did not like all of those people telling *me* what to do, either. After all, I had gone to college. I had taken two semesters of ROTC! And besides, they were all a bunch of hillbillies and drunks. Obviously, the Army was the problem, so I did what I had to in order to get a medical discharge.

Next I enrolled in another college, without the GI bill but with renewed promises to my parents. However, they said that this was my last chance. They were not going to pay anymore if I did not make it there. I lasted there one quarter. During that time I lost two jobs because I was too stoned to perform, attended classes about one-fourth of the time, and fought with and stole from my roommates. I was out of money, in trouble with my roommates, and in danger of being placed on academic probation again. Of course, I believed that my dilemma was due to the defectiveness of my employers, roommates, and the college.

My parents had reached the end of their rope. Even I had begun to suspect that my chemical use was getting out of hand. My suspicions began when one of my roommates, who was drunk at the time, suggested that I get help for my drug problem. Of course I had some suggestions for him. Among others, I suggested that if he wanted to see someone who really had a problem, he ought to look in a mirror. That was my defensive external reaction. But my internal reaction was, *If he can see something in me, and he's drunk, maybe there really is something to see. Maybe I'm not doing such a good job of hiding it after all.*

I was at a point where I had to quickly think of a way out of this unhealthy situation. My environment was dragging me down, I thought. Suddenly I thought of the perfect solution to all of my problems. I would make another geographical escape. This time, however, it would be to a *Christian* college. After all, this would get me out of this terrible situation that obviously was the source of my difficulties. In addition, my parents would still pay because they also believed that my geographical location was the problem. Finally, the particular college I had in mind had a lifestyle statement, the signing of which meant I was not going to use alcohol or drugs (among other things).

I'll attend this school and then I won't be able to use. After all, I'll have signed a statement. What a plan! I mailed in my application and included the best phony statement of faith you ever saw. I was accepted in the middle of the year. When I got there in February, I signed the lifestyle statement . . . and I used chemicals like crazy! Why? Because I was chemically dependent. Hear me, please! That does not excuse my behavior, but it does explain it. I had lost control of my chemical use and my life. My "yes" did not mean "yes," and my "no" did not mean "no." Feeling bad about what I was doing (and I did), promising not to do it anymore (which I did), and even putting myself in an environment where all of the pressure was *toward* abstinence, were not sufficient incentives or resources to enable me to follow through with my commitment.

There are two reasons, then, why people use chemicals: (1) They decide to, and (2) They can't decide not to. I had crossed the line from reason number 1 to reason number 2. My later awareness of my condition did not justify my past behavior or get me out of its consequences. Indeed, when my needs became evident to me, I was able to undertake a course of growth. Through the process, I was also able to learn some things about pain that were extremely helpful in many areas of my life, not just with regard to my chemical use.

The Real Danger

The real danger with chemicals is not that they don't work. The real problem is that they do, at least while the effects of the chemical are present. If you feel sad and you do not want to, chemicals will numb your sadness. If you are shy, you may find out that chemicals will suppress your inhibitions. If you are uptight, chemicals will help you unwind. There are chemical substances with which you can manipulate your mood to any point on the emotional spectrum. Chemicals are dependable, which means that they will always do what you ask of them to the extent to which they are able. Later I will discuss some of their limitations.

Two Crucial Concerns

This raises two crucial concerns. First, chemicals are sometimes more dependable than people when it comes to helping with emotional pain. It should not be this way, but you cannot count on people to help. Sometimes your family, minister, friends, church, or fellow employees let you down by not being there when you need them. Sometimes you might come away from an attempt to ask for support from someone with more pain than when you first went. People do not always mean what they say or always follow through. They do not always know what to say, or they may be unintentionally abusive by pretending to know.

Still, chemical use is not justified just because any of the above situations is true, but at times chemical use might be viewed as a more helpful alternative than a particular relationship. Chemicals will not let you down. They will numb the emotional pain that may have motivated you to seek support in the first place. Through this you may learn the tragic lesson I have been discussing: chemical use works. Especially in the early stages of use, chemicals seem to work every time. Therefore, you may become willing to pay some prices in your relationships with others (who do not always help) to keep your relationship with chemicals (which have been helpful up to this point). You lie a little, withdraw a little, and grow a little further away from people who used to be close. But that's OK. If you feel lonely, using a chemical will help.

Let me clarify something at this point. Over the long run, healthy relationships with Christ, family members, and those in the body of Christ *are* dependable. They are messy, risky (meaning they call for vulnerability) relationships, and they take time. Healthy relationships do not just happen; they take work and investment. Chemicals are neat, easy, quick, cheap (initially), and they work while the user is under their influence.

My second concern is that while a person is learning that chemical use is a dependable solution to problems, it is possible for further problems to occur without being noticed. Not only does chemical use take the place of other resources in a person's life, but it also numbs the pain that should be there because of the price being paid. When you have exchanged your relationship with someone important for a relationship with chemicals, you *should* feel emotional pain. When your performance at work is suffering and the threat of being fired is there, you *should* feel pain. When your grades are plummeting because of partying instead of studying, you *should* feel pain. When you are spending money on alcohol or drugs that you need or want for other things, you *should* feel pain. When people are hurt, angry, or fed up with you for failing to keep commitments unless they suit your purposes, you *should* feel pain.

The pain is healthy. Pain is there as a signal to show you how you have compromised, changed, or hurt others, and what you have paid to keep your chemical use. Pain points to the fact that you need help and support in order to change your unhealthy way of life. But the *danger of chemical use* is that at the same time your use is creating these painful circumstances, it is also numbing the pain.

Jesi Learns about Pain

The normal human response to pain is to avoid it. One day a few years ago, I was sitting on our sofa drinking from a stoneware mug that was very hot from the coffee inside. Jesi (our third daughter out of four) was just learning to walk and talk at the same time. She toddled over to me, tugged on my sleeve, reached for the mug, and asked for a drink. "Hot!" I warned. "Drink, drink," she persisted. "Hot, hot," I countered. "Drink, drink, drink," she insisted. "Hot, hot, hot!" I insisted right back.

Suddenly I had two realizations. First, it occurred to me that we were both having a tantrum together. I could tell because I was raising my voice and stamping my feet just like Jesi. The second insight, however, was more profound. I realized that Jesi did not know what *hot* meant. She had no experience of hot. Why, someday she might be headed for something hot and despite my cries of "Hot!" she could get seriously burned for lack of understanding a word. I decided that this present situation represented a relatively safe and painless (yet painful enough) opportunity to demonstrate the meaning of hot.

I extended my arm to bring the mug within her reach. She grasped it. Now if you or I had grabbed the mug, we would have immediately recognized that our hand was burning. Instantly, without a thought, we would have jerked our hand away. But not Jesi, much to my guilty surprise. No, Jesi just gave the mug a dirty look. Then she gave me a dirtier look. I imagined in my mind a fourteen-year-old Jesi using dope to fulfill the plot for revenge hatched on this fateful day. She removed her hand from the mug as tears welled up in her eyes. At the moment I saw the pain register on her little face, I said, "Hot!" Hot suddenly took on meaning for this tiny explorer.

I decided to see how deeply she had learned the lesson. I set the mug on an end table and left the room. When I peeked into the room, Jesi had already forgotten the lesson and was stalking the coffee. I was encouraged, however, because she was blowing on it from quite a distance away. As she reached for the mug, I said "Hot!" from across the room. She jerked her hand back, turned around, and almost tumbled away from the coffee. Brilliant? Exceptional? No. Normal! The normal human response to pain is to avoid it, to escape it.

Yet for some reason, a person who is using chemicals can be losing his relationships with family members, experiencing legal problems, spending money needed for essentials on chemical use, losing friends, in trouble at work, and experiencing other problems that *should* be causing him pain. And that pain *should* be telling him to take a look at his life. And it *should* be instructing him to make the changes necessary to eliminate the pain. Yet the same chemical use that causes the pain numbs the pain! *That's* the problem with chemical use. It is why chemical use can progress to chemical dependency.

Obscured by Three Factors

Chapter 3 is about the chemical dependency process in which a person progresses from abstinence to dependency. However, a number of factors have the potential to muddy the waters. Understanding them now will be helpful later when seeking to understand the person who is becoming dependent. One of them is the *rate* factor. The dependency process happens at different rates for different people. Comparing our situation with someone whose situation is worse and concluding that we do not have a problem is very easy to do.

For this reason, stereotypes are dangerous. Only 3 percent of all alcoholics, for instance, are in skid row settings. Yet that is what most people think of when you say the word *alcoholic*. The other 97 percent are moms and dads, teachers, lawyers, doctors, pastors, cheerleaders, or Sunday school superintendents—you know, family types who are still holding down their jobs. As a matter of fact, family relationships deteriorate long before jobs because of our emphasis on our jobs as the validation of our worth.

The question to ask is not whether your chemical use and its consequences resemble that of others who are using. The questions that need to be asked are "why" questions. Why do you use? Not what, when, or how much, but why? If the "why" is to manipulate your emotions instead of going toward healthy, redemptive relationships, you are in dangerous waters. And why are you willing to pay the spiritual, psychological, emotional, physical, social, and financial prices that you are paying to keep your chemical use? If you are willing to continue to use in a way that causes negative consequences, the "why" is that you have a problem and need help.

Another factor is that of *denial*. Denial is a normal human response to situations in which the emotional gravity is too overwhelming to confront all at once. God has given us an automatic, built-in buffer to help us move on from the initial experience of pain to a place where we can cope with and even grow from it. We experience denial when a friend or family member dies. We say, "I can't believe it, I just saw him!" We feel numb. If we were able to feel all of the ramifications of the loss at one time, the results would be disastrous. So God gives us this built-in mechanism to take us through the experience. We begin at the initial experience of loss and grow to being able to withstand its entire impact without losing our ability to function in life.

This kind of denial is unconscious. But the kind of denial that is involved in the chemical dependency process is *conscious*. The danger for the chemical user (or anyone who consciously denies the truth of pain and problems) is that conscious denial over a prolonged period of time results in delusion. You see, the chemical user loses someone very special to him through the chemical dependency process. He loses himself. To see all at once the prices he has paid, the people he has hurt, the person he has become, would have devastating spiritual, psychological, and emotional consequences. Denial saves the user from that disaster. While it is saving him from one disaster, it is causing him to be swallowed up by another—the progression into chemical dependency—secure in the belief that someone or something else is the problem.

The final factor is *delusion*. Delusion is the distorted perception of reality, a totally unrealistic, twisted view of what is real. Delusion is the end result of denial. In the case of the chemically dependent person and those who love him, it is a wall of defenses that protects them from the truth, and thus, from overcoming the problem. At its best, delusion exists initially to convince others that everything is fine and to fix blame for the problem away from the chemical user. At its worst, delusion succeeds in convincing the dependent person himself.

Romans 1:22 says, "Professing to be wise, they became fools." These are not foolish people who know they are fools. They have simply professed their wisdom, and their pride and pretense have led them to be fools. However, they cannot see it. Verse 28 mentions the "debased mind," the mind that is no mind at all, the mind that cannot tell the difference. Delusion is the ultimate end of pretending.

Remember This Lesson!

The most frustrating, yet probably the most helpful, lesson I had to learn in trying to help chemically dependent people is that their delusion is sincere. They are no longer making excuses to throw people off their trails. They believe the excuses themselves. The end result is a belief system that stays intact despite negative consequences, pain, and confrontation by loved ones that are designed to help. Their belief enables them to continue to use chemicals to mask the problems the chemical use itself is causing. It prevents them from seeing the devastating effects of their chemical dependency upon themselves, those they love, and those who love them.

Delusion is why chemically dependent people promise to quit using, do so, and then return to using after they have sufficiently "proved" to themselves and others that there is no problem. Delusion is why questions like "Can't you see what you are doing to yourself (me, the family)?" are not helpful. They *cannot* see. They cannot see how they are hurting their health, their education, their job, or their bank account either. Statements such as "Jesus is the way" do not usually work either. Jesus *is* the way. He is the most profound reality there is. But chemically dependent people cannot even see simple realities, such as the fact that their harsh words hurt their children, or that they could kill themselves if they drive drunk, or that the money being spent on alcohol is needed for groceries.

A Terrible Yet Wonderful Realization

I would like to close this chapter with an illustration of delusion and the part it plays in the chemical dependency process. While a counselor at an inpatient center, I had a client I will call John. John had received numerous DWI (driving while intoxicated) tickets. He had lost his license after the second ticket but kept driving anyway, which meant that the remaining tickets were aggravated charges. One day in group therapy, I asked him how it was that he had gotten so many DWIs. He began his story.

"It seems to me," he said, "that every time I drove I got a ticket!" I asked him why. He said that it took him a while but he had finally figured it out. "I'm a problem driver," he chirped proudly. His solution to the traffic tickets, therefore, was to quit driving. At this point in the conversation I laughed and gave him a perplexed glance, as if to say, "Do you really believe that?" He got a hurt expression on his face that I will never forget. And then it struck me. John had noticed that things were not going very well in his life. He stepped back in an attempt to diagnose the problem. His sincere diagnosis was that his real problem was his driving. Therefore, he eliminated it.

I asked him, once again, how he got in a treatment center. He told the group that one night he was drunk and walking home from a party. He had to walk to and from parties, work, and so forth, because walking was the solution to his driving problems. On his way home, he stole a four-hundred-pound tool kit from the back of a pickup truck. When the police pulled up, he pretended that he could not figure out how the tool kit got off the truck. He did not know how his fingerprints got on it either, or how the tool kit had gotten so far away from the truck. They arrested him anyway and charged him with felony theft.

At that point in the story, I asked him, "What did you do then, stop walking?" A confused expression came over his face and he exclaimed, "What?" I said, "Well, you were driving, received tickets, and quit driving. I was wondering if after being arrested while walking you decided to quit walking." "What are you talking about?" he complained. I came back with another question. "Did you ever get any traffic tickets when you were not drinking?" I asked. He thought for a moment and said, "No." "Well," I pressed, "did you ever get busted for felony theft when you were not drinking?" Again his answer was no. "Then," I challenged, "maybe the real problem is your drinking." He looked at me with a confused, then thoughtful look, and then with the expression of someone who suddenly found a treasure that was in the open all along. "It is!" he cried.

He was suddenly free. The truth was there all along. He had mysteriously forgotten that he was drunk every time he got a ticket. He had forgotten that he had been drunk or too hung over to go to work each time he had lost a job. He had forgotten that he had been drunk and threatening to his mother when his parents kicked him out of the house. His response to these new insights was not one of self-condemnation. He did not say, "Oh no, what a lousy drunk I am." Instead, he realized that it was not the driving that was the problem. John also realized it was not the walking, the police, the probation officer, the parents, the boss, the chemical dependency counselor, or anything else that was the problem. He had waited so long for all of those other things to straighten out so his life would start working. The wait was over. He was chemically dependent. He was the problem. Something could be done about that now, and he felt hopeful.

What a revelation it is to see that you are responsible for yourself, your behavior, the problems it causes, and for seeking help to meet your needs. When it is always someone or something other than yourself that is the problem, you are a victim at the mercy of external circumstances. The realization of the need for help and the willingness to ask for it mean that help is not far behind. *Now* maybe some of the questions such as, "Can't you see what you are doing?" can be heard. "Jesus is the way" is even a viable alternative to someone who realizes that his way is not working.

All I did with John was spend a little time accepting him and using simple questions aimed at the truth to poke holes in his wall of delusion. He began to recover, by the way, and even decided to get his life from God. This wonderful process of spiritual, emotional, and psychological growth began with John's simple, yet difficult to reach, realization that he was chemically dependent and in need of help.

3

The Power of Chemicals

In 1 Corinthians 6:12, Paul said, "All things are lawful for me, but all things are not helpful. All things are lawful for me, but I will not be brought under the power of any." Paul demonstrated in this passage that the motivation for behavior on the part of the Christian is not whether it is lawful, but whether it is helpful and whether we become slaves through the process. In the following pages you will see the process of being brought under the power of chemicals.

Light and Heavy Emotions

Examples of light emotions are love, joy, excitement, anticipation of a positive experience, and happiness. I call them light because a person can carry a lot of them as if they were feathers. Light feelings do not weigh us down, and because they are light, they are easy to give away. People like them, want them, and accept them from one another. When my babies were born, I called many people on the telephone, some very late in the night, in order to give away my light emotions. No one said, "Why did you call me in the middle of the night?" They all said, "Congratulations! Thanks for sharing your good news."

Examples of heavy emotions are hurt, sadness, embarrassment, fear, jealousy, anger, and remorse. They weigh us down. They get in the way. We cannot continue to carry a lot of them without experiencing negative consequences in our lives. I can sometimes detect people who are carrying heavy emotions just by looking at them. They walk as if carrying a heavy load, their eyes and heads appear weighted down, their energy level is low, and it is sometimes hard for them to move. I have seldom counseled anyone who began problem chemical use at normal. Most began from a heavy place they had grown accustomed to thinking was normal.

Heavy emotions are also hard to give away. No one else wants our heavy emotions; they have enough of their own. Fellow Christians quote us Bible verses and tell us not to feel what we already do. Quoting Philippians 4:6, "Be anxious for nothing," to a person who is already anxious will just make that person feel guilty for not feeling how he or she "should." They will thereby have to carry both the heavy emotions of guilt *and* anxiety. A more appropriate response to the anxious person is the assurance that you will stand by him or her no matter how heavy it gets.

Churches and Christian families will not accept a person's anger, but we will accept "righteous indignation." What a game! Society accepts anger (strong) from men but not from women. Society accepts fear or sadness (weak) from women but not from men. What a lie! Men feel hurt and afraid and women feel angry.

We are conditioned in families, churches, and society to look like we feel or do not feel a certain way in order to earn approval, pacify others, or prove our spirituality. So we expose only those emotions we think will make us acceptable and stuff the rest deep inside to come out later. They will come out crooked if we do not deal with them in a way that is straight. Depression (frozen heavy emotions) is probably the most common result of attempting to carry a lot of heavy emotions, followed closely by stress-related physical illnesses.

John's Experiment

In this chapter, let's name our hypothetical person John and take him through the process of going from abstinence to dependency. His decision to use a chemical substance may be his response to a variety of situations. Perhaps John is experiencing some heavy emotions and lacks the skills and relationships with which to handle them constructively. Perhaps he believes that chemical use will somehow gain him the love and acceptance of those with whom he uses. He will discover that chemical use will numb the painful feeling of conditional love from those most important to him. Perhaps he feels insecure or inadequate. Chemicals will obscure those sensations and maybe even give him a false sense of security.

When a person chooses to use chemicals for the first time, it is an experiment, just like in chemistry class. The purpose of any experiment is to discover something new or to prove or disprove someone else's theory. Most people who use a chemical for the first time do so to see if using will do for them what someone else said it would. Once John uses, then the experiment is over.

I have heard parents say, "My son/daughter is into heavy experimentation with drugs." There is no such thing as heavy experimentation. When the results are known, the only reason left to repeat the experiment is that the experimenter *liked* the results. In this case, the experiment got John high. The chemicals manipulated his emotions into the "light" range.

When the effect of the chemicals wore off, John returned to normal. If John started from a heavy place, he returned to that heavy place.

Learning Internal Control

Even though the initial experiment may have been to discover if someone else's theory was correct, John will have also learned that he can control how he feels easily, quickly, inexpensively, and with relatively little relationship risk (at least on the front end). This is such an unhealthy, even dangerous, lesson to learn.

Genesis 1:26 says, "Then God said, 'Let Us make man in Our image, according to Our likeness; let them *have dominion*.'" Verse 28 continues with, "Then God blessed them, and God said to them, 'Be *fruitful* and *multiply*; *fill* the earth and *subdue* it; *have dominion*'" (italics mine). Have dominion, be fruitful, multiply, fill, subdue, these are all words that communicate the concept of control. They indicate one of the ways in which man is created in God's own image: God is a controller, and man (by God's command) is a controller as well. God made all things and put man in charge of everything (except for a single tree in the middle of the garden).

John, you, and I are controllers. We like to be in charge; it fits with how we were built. We can control what we say, how we dress, what we eat, when we rise or retire, who we choose as friends, how fast we drive, and who we worship. God has built us to make choices. Through John's choice in step 1, John has learned that he can control how he feels (internal), along with all of the other things (external) he already controls. Learning that he can manipulate his emotions with a chemical substance is the beginning of John's chemical dependency.

Appropriate Social Use

Society's definition of the appropriate social user is a person whose chemical use causes no harmful consequences to himself or others. Any chemical use that breaks society's law is inappropriate. Any chemical use that causes the "weaker brother" to stumble is inappropriate.

An appropriate social user, should his alcohol or drug use cause a problem (about which the user would be notified by heavy emotional signals), would choose to eliminate the chemical use necessary to eliminate the problem. He would choose to adjust his use to accommodate his life (job, school, finances, relationships). But the chemically dependent person chooses to adjust his life to accommodate his use. This is the choice that was made by John.

Taking Control

John learned that he could control his feelings with a chemical. He learned that chemicals are capable of causing pleasure, or at least a temporary respite from a heavy emotional place. He probably also learned that all of those terrible things he was told as a kid would happen if he used *did not* happen. Chemical use produced lightness, not pain. John decides to exercise this control.

John may simply be seeking to repeat an experience he enjoyed. However, he may be consciously choosing instead to manipulate his emotions. For instance, let's say that John has gotten home from work and feels frustrated about the job, angry at a colleague, or guilty for having to work so much. The act of taking a drink (smoking a joint, popping a pill) will have a numbing effect on his emotional pain. If he does this intentionally, his use constitutes abuse because those feelings of frustration, anger, or guilt are valuable signals. They are there to drive John to do something about the problem that is causing him to feel the heavy emotions. Healthy choices have the potential of returning John to an emotionally normal state.

When he takes his chemical to unwind, the feelings are numbed, the situation or relationship remains the same, and John has missed a golden opportunity. He has ignored the signal and will not make the choice by which he can benefit from the situation or grow in the relationship. Not only that, but tomorrow he will return to work. Nothing will be different, neither there nor in him, except that he has reinforced the lesson learned concerning the power to control emotions with chemicals. If he chooses to drink to unwind, his drinking *will* help him unwind. The chemical dependency foundation has been laid.

Beginning to Lose Ground

To make matters worse, what if, during the time in which John was under the influence of chemicals, he said something or did something that goes against his values or is inconsistent with his identity? Contrary to popular stereotypical belief, chemically dependent people *do* feel remorse for their behavior. He might have said a hurtful thing to his spouse, children, or parents. He might have stolen something from a motel room. Perhaps he acted foolishly in a social setting, and his spouse or children are humiliated. Or maybe someone said something hurtful to John (of course, under the influence of chemicals, he will not feel hurt). When the effects of the chemical wear off, he will not return to normal. He will experience a heavy emotion such as remorse, embarrassment, or hurt.

Consider this example of something I did when I was using that I never would have done if I had been sober, because it was against my values. When I was in college I dated a young woman I was crazy about. We had an arrangement that neither of us would go out with anyone else. One Friday night she went on a date with another man. I found out about it and felt jealous and afraid. I got drunk, went to her dorm room, and hit her with the back of my hand. The next day when I sobered up, I remembered what I had done. Consequently, I felt a number of heavy emotions. I still felt jealous and afraid, as I did before the incident. I also felt sad and angry that she had broken her commitment, angry at myself for acting the way I did, more afraid than before that I was losing her, and guilty for the way I had acted.

Those emotions were there to tell me something about my behavior. They did. They were also there to motivate me to apologize to my girlfriend and take whatever steps were needed to ensure that it would not happen again. If I had done that, I would have returned to an emotional normal and the relationship might have resumed a positive direction.

I chose instead to say, "If you had not broken your commitment to me, I would not have hit you." This focused on her as the cause for my inappropriate, violent behavior and allowed me to deny the presence of my heavy emotions. I was acting as if I did not feel the way I really felt, as if there were a good enough reason to hit someone. I made an excuse and acted as if she were the one who should feel guilty, not I. I simply pretended to feel normal.

As a result, I got to keep all of my heavy emotions.

Pretending That What Is Real Isn't

Now John has the same choices as I did when he acts in ways inconsistent with *his* values. He can go toward relationships and resolve problems in response to his heavy emotions. If he chooses this alternative, he will be doing the emotional and relational work necessary to return to normal. On the other hand, John may choose another alternative. He may choose to hide his pain and keep his problem behavior. He does this by blaming someone or something else for his problems.

He may say, "If you didn't nag so much, I wouldn't go out so much," or "I've had such a hard day at work. If only you knew what kind of people I have to deal with all day long, you wouldn't get upset over a few lousy drinks," or "You can't blame me for acting this way. I had a terrible childhood." The list goes on and on. If John chooses the latter alternative, he is trying to give the impression that he does not feel the way he really feels or that he is not responsible for what he does. He is storing his heavy emotions inside and putting up a wall of excuses to keep people from seeing them.

I hope you are beginning to realize the extreme importance of our families and churches being the kinds of places where people know that they do not have to pretend. In order to stay emotionally healthy, we all must be able to share all of our problems and feelings out of the knowledge that love and acceptance are not conditional, not based on our lack of problems.

Two Steps Backward, One Step Forward

The next time John uses, he starts from an emotional place that is heavier than the first time. When the effects of the chemical wear off, he returns to that place, *unless* he does something that results in more heavy emotions.

If this is the case, John again has a choice. He can choose to deal with his emotions in the context of those relationships God has provided, or he can stuff the emotion and hide the pain with an excuse. If he chooses the latter course, the emotional level he calls normal will have once again been lowered. His wall of excuses will also have grown a little thicker and harder to penetrate. In addition, he will be set up to be relieved by more chemical use.

Welcome to Chemical Dependency

Continuing to make these kinds of behavior choices, while using chemicals to numb heavy emotional signals, will result in chemical dependency. Let's look at the entire process.

First John learned to control his emotions with the use of chemicals. Next he chose to exercise the control he learned he had in doing this. Then came the point at which John lost control of his chemical use. People cross that line at different points in their using history, and it is different for each person. However, it will happen if the process goes on uninterrupted.

In reality, John is trapped. He must continue to invest in the course he has chosen to justify past investments. Have you ever been trapped like this? You may think not. But have you ever been placed on hold on the telephone? After five minutes you think, *I don't have time to be sitting on hold! I need to hang up.* Then you think, *I can't hang up! If I hang up, I'll have to call later and I might be put on hold from the beginning again. Anyway, I've already waited five minutes. A couple more minutes won't hurt.* But after five more minutes you are more trapped than before. Now, you have ten minutes to rescue instead of just five.

Serving the Gift

There are many of these kinds of traps in life: relationships, jobs, projects, and so forth. I was trapped by a 1972 Ford LTD once. The car was given to us for almost nothing at a time when we badly needed it. When it hit 100,000 miles, things began to break, I replaced the muffler, and that cost around $100. Then I discovered the brakes were unsafe. Another $150. At that point I thought, *I've got to get rid of this car. This car is sucking me dry!* Then I thought, *I can't get rid of this car. I've got $250 sunk into it. I have to keep it.* Then the alternator went bad. Another $125. Then I thought, *This is it! I have to ditch this car.* Then I thought, *I can't do that! I have $375 in this car. I have to get my money's worth out of these new parts, and there is no way I'm going to let someone else benefit from them. Besides, this is probably all I'll have to replace.*

The promise that things will get better and the need to rescue past investments make for a dangerous combination, even when the numbing effect of chemicals is absent. Add chemicals and the trap is more deadly still.

Answers That Leave Us out of the Pain

John is chemically dependent and chemical use is the controlling factor in his life. Without his use, John is in an incredibly heavy emotional pit. That is why he will think you are a lunatic if you suggest that he quit using. You are asking him to give up what he thinks is probably his last means to get back near normal. In addition, to give up this course would constitute an admission that he has wasted past investments and things are not going to get better. He is also sincerely deluded, and he is unable to see what his chemical use is doing to himself and others.

That is also why it is not enough at this point to get John to quit using. He needs to relearn long-forgotten living skills and learn others for the first time. He needs to come to grips with his emotional pain and problems. He also must get a clear picture of his delusion and the defense mechanisms that contribute to his staying dysfunctional (*dysfunctional* simply means functioning in a way that is not healthy and does not work in relationships).

If John came into a relationship with Jesus Christ, many of us would breathe a huge sigh of relief and say, "Whew! It's over." *Wrong!* It has just begun. Without healthy relationships in which to learn new, functional living skills (discipleship), and without a healthy environment in which John can see himself in the light of truth, his conversion, sincere as it may be, will amount to a spiritual high. And it is bound to wear off sooner or later. When that happens, John will crash back into the emotional pit with the likelihood of turning to the one thing he *knows* will manipulate his emotional state in a "light" direction. Then, those of us who thought it was over when John met Jesus will say, "Well, he must not have really come to Christ in the first place." Actually, what has happened is that his old, "dependable" chemical cure has refilled the gap that should have been filled with new living skills and redemptive relationships.

Like Knocking Over Dominoes

In the chemically dependent person, we see an individual who has clung to his chemical resource at the expense of other resources in his life. We see someone who has self-medicated away profound feelings of guilt about his actions and shame about himself. He is a person who has acquired a lifestyle and relationships that support chemical use, and a mindset that protects him from seeing the person he has become and the pain he has caused others.

A final note before I bring this chapter to a close. I have described the process by which a person becomes chemically dependent. Understanding the *order* in which the process usually takes place will be very helpful when we finally begin to learn how to help the chemically dependent person and others who have been affected.

Many areas of life become, or already are, dysfunctional when a person is involved in the dependency process. *Spiritually*, the dependent person is turning to chemicals as his god. Alcohol and/or drugs are his source of well-being, his main resource for coping with life.

In Romans 6, Paul described a process that resembles very much what I have been describing. He said in verse 16, "Do you not know that to whom you present yourselves slaves to obey, you are that one's slaves whom you obey?" and again in verse 19, "You presented your members as slaves of uncleanness, and of lawlessness leading to more lawlessness." And read verse 21 closely: "What fruit did you have then in the things of which you are now ashamed?"

The chemically dependent person has had a puny chemical god, or he has been god of his own life. Not having needed help or input, he has controlled and decided everything without paying attention to the price being paid. In turning to these gods, he has turned to weak gods to provide what they cannot. Consequently, he has become addicted, which has caused negative consequences in his life and in the lives of those who are in relationships with him.

Emotionally, the chemically dependent individual has denied his pain and hidden his shame with excuses, rationalizations, blaming, minimizing, bargaining, and promises to do better next time. *Psychologically*, he has developed ways to justify to himself and others that wrong is right. These defense mechanisms have hardened into a concrete wall of delusion. *Physically*, his lifestyle has not been conducive to health. His heart, lungs, liver, brain, and other organs may have been damaged permanently, even fatally, depending upon the kind, amount, and duration of chemical use.

An important point to recognize, yet one that is extremely obscure, is that the areas I have just described as being affected are usually affected in the order in which I described them: spiritual, emotional, psychological, and physical. However, they must be addressed in reverse order. This is very hard to remember in a religious community that continues to focus on giving spiritual answers, even though many people are not asking spiritual questions. More often than not, dysfunction, needs, and pain in each area tend to mask the need for help in the area preceding it. This progression must be remembered when attempting to help in ways that are really effective.

4

"Saving" a Family Member While Losing a Family

For every one chemically dependent person, it is estimated that there are four or five other people whose lives are being affected in various and harmful ways. That is why chemical dependency is sometimes referred to as a family illness. Three basic ingredients must be present in order for someone to be affected by someone else's chemical dependency. When these are present, there *will* be negative consequences. How much a person is affected, and in what ways, is directly related to the degree that these ingredients are present.

Three Necessary Ingredients

First, you have to *care* about the chemically dependent person. If you love someone in the clutches of chemical dependency, chances are you will be affected in various ways on the inside and the outside. People who do not care are not affected internally, even though they may experience negative external consequences (financial, for instance).

The degree to which these effects harm you depends upon the second ingredient: *unawareness* or *ill-awareness*. Caring for people will be affected when someone they love becomes chemically dependent. However, caring people who do not understand chemical dependency are likely to be affected in more harmful ways than those who understand the problem, because they neglect to pursue healthful ways to help the situation. More often than not, they pursue unhealthy avenues that actually contribute to the problem they are trying to solve.

The third ingredient, *shame* about yourself, compounds the situation even more. Shame is the feeling or belief that you lack value and are defective as a person. Shame leads to attempting to acquire value points from your performance and the performance of others in your life. It also leads to a tendency to deny reality, because any reality that has a negative reflection upon you shames you. The contribution of shame to the destruction of both the dependent person and the relationships with loved ones is vast and complicated. We will look at this more closely in chapter 6.

A Little Leaven Leavens the Whole Lump

Chemical dependency has a general impact on those who love the dependent person. When someone in a family begins to rely on chemical substances to deal with reality, those who have relationships with that person may react in several ways. For a relationship between people to be meaningful, there must be emotional involvement and the investment of time and effort. Chemical dependency is like someone having a relationship with a chemical partner. As that relationship develops, family members or friends (anyone who simply cares) begin to feel a distance between themselves and the chemical user. The energy and effort of that person is being poured into a relationship with chemicals. The emotional connection between the user and those who care is being short-circuited.

As the dependent person focuses more and more on chemicals to meet certain needs, he will become a less efficient, less productive, less responsible member of the systems to which he belongs: family, peers, school, education, church. Two very serious consequences happen in systems that contain people who are becoming dysfunctional. Before I discuss them, allow me to set the stage.

A Healthy Family System

In a healthy, functional family system, people feel safe and comfortable. This does not mean that there are never problems; it means that they know they are loved and accepted without strings. They are affirmed in the fact that they are capable, special, and needed; and they know they will not be left alone to face painful realities. Relationships (respect, honesty, communication, risk-taking, trust, forgiveness, acceptance, love, emotional investment) go in all directions.

Losing Someone to Chemicals

As one family member begins to channel energy into a relationship with chemicals and away from other family members, their relationships turn toward that one family member.

The chemical user and his behavior become the focus of the family. Family members, therefore, begin to channel their emotions and energy toward the dependent person. They receive very little in return, and other relationships are put on hold. The system becomes dysfunctional and will become increasingly so unless this process is interrupted and reversed.

A family that once radiated comfort and safety, if it ever did (most families I counsel never did), is now a painful, uncomfortable place to be. In an effort to make the situation a little less painful and a little more comfortable, family members react by adjusting to accommodate the dysfunction.

Adjusting Thoughts and Feelings

Now we come to those two significant consequences. First, instead of being able to channel its energy into convincing its members that they are loved and accepted unconditionally, that they are capable and needed, and that they are not alone, this family becomes *psycho-emotionally reactive*. Psycho-emotionally reactive simply means that people consciously or unconsciously adjust how they think or feel in order to make sense of a difficult situation. Often these many reactions seem to be "all or nothing" in nature. For instance, family members tend to either ignore harmful behavior or dwell on it, overlook things or become super-detectives who track down every clue, hide their emotions, or blame others for them. They become apathetic about the painful actions and attitudes of others, or they become very rigid and rule-oriented in an attempt to control others.

Pain will do that to you, especially in a system like this where pain and stress are increasing at the same time that formerly supportive relationships are crumbling. Studies in the area of professional burnout, for instance, indicate that organizations that create an environment where stress increases while support decreases (giving employees responsibility but no authority) burn out employees. Those where support is increased in direct proportion to the stress keep healthier employees for a longer period of time. The same situation occurs in families.

Family members choose not to trust because it hurts too much to be let down continually. Since mutual need-meeting has ceased, selfishness in an attempt to survive replaces any self-lessness to build others. Direct confrontation and honesty bring problems and pain to the surface and must be punished and replaced by unhealthy, manipulative forms of communication.

Honesty is extinguished in many ways. One common method is to blame the honest person for causing the turmoil by being honest. In other words, the harmful behavior and attitude of a family member are not really the problem. The problem is the person who says out loud that there is a problem. This makes the honest person feel responsible for causing Mom's headaches, Dad's outbursts of anger, or a sibling's running away. Over a period of time, family members get the message that honesty and reality do not matter, that what really matters are people's impressions and opinions. Only the expression of feelings and opinions that do not make waves is acceptable in this family. The integrity of the family members gets exchanged for a false peace.

Another way to extinguish honesty is to justify continually or explain away the harmful, hurtful behavior of a family member. Whenever another member of the family takes the risk of confronting the unhealthy situation, others in the system rush to make excuses for it. Eventually, the honest person may just give up.

A "do not talk" rule develops that says that it is not OK to talk about how family members feel, what they see, and how they are being affected. Talking within the family, to the neighbors, with the relatives, or with church members is never allowed. The personal integrity of individuals deteriorates as they stuff their emotions and insights. They begin to support or at least ignore on the outside that with which they disagree on the inside.

What is the bottom line? Spiritually, emotionally, and psychologically the family has ceased to function like a family. Physically, they settle for living together, eating together, going places together, watching television together. They define *family* in terms of physical geography instead of relational intimacy. Family members increasingly feel that they are *not* loved and accepted, or at least not without a lot of strings. They sense that they are not capable or needed, and they feel isolated from the rest of the family and those outside the family as well. Their shame about themselves increases, they develop a pattern of denying painful reality, and they acquire a variety of unhealthy relationship skills. Eventually, they take all of this into new relationships.

All of this results from negotiating away reality—with good intentions. Loved ones believe that all of the compromising will help the dependent person. Compromising with illness, however, cannot possibly help. The efforts of family members to alleviate family pain actually perpetuate the cause of the pain in the first place. The first consequence of system dysfunction, then, is that members of the family become psycho-emotionally reactive.

Trying Harder

The second consequence is that family members become *functionally reactive*. Functionally reactive means that family members adjust how they act in order to fix someone else's problem. In general, this is quite a normal phenomenon. Suppose, for example, that one day while jogging I slip by accident on a roller skate and break my leg. At the hospital the doctor puts my leg in a cast with the following instructions, "Go home and lie down for six weeks so that your leg can heal properly." I might feel relieved to have a rest, bored to have nothing to do, or financially insecure to not be working. I might follow the doctor's instructions or I might not.

More important, however, are the effects of my dysfunction (broken leg) upon my family members and others with whom I have relationships. I have become, almost instantly, a less efficient, less productive, less contributing member of my family system. I may not have an income, so my wife will have to get a job. I may not be able to take out the garbage, so one of my daughters will have to do it. I will not be able to mow the lawn, so the neighbor kid will be hired for the job. The elders of our church, of whom I am one, may decide to meet at my house so I will not miss the meeting. Someone might tape sermons for me on the days I cannot attend the church service. I am less able to function, so people who care about me decide to function more. But I am enabled to function less, *because* people decide to function more.

This is true in a family where there is chemical dependency as well. As the dependent person channels more energy, effort, and emotions into a relationship with chemicals, he becomes a less efficient, less productive, less contributing member of the systems of which he is a part. His dysfunction (chemical dependency) in those systems will have functional ramifications upon family members and others who care. Instead of contributing to the financial needs of all the family members, money is being funneled into his effort to maintain a chemical lifestyle. A chemical lifestyle for teenagers includes the use of alcohol/drugs propped up by concerts, stereos, video games, beer parties, and using paraphernalia. A chemical lifestyle for adults includes the use of alcohol/drugs propped up by football games, card games, bachelor parties, built-in bars, liquor cabinets, and doctor's prescriptions.

When the family begins to feel the financial pressure being placed upon them by their loved one's pursuit of chemicals, another family member may need to find other income to compensate. If the chemical user becomes irresponsible in his chores or household tasks, other family members will have to do more in order to take up the slack. As a chemical user becomes more incapable of functioning normally and feels guiltier, he may avoid friends or fellow church members. Therefore, family members often choose to lie or make excuses for his absence.

Chemical use might adversely affect the user's job performance—lateness or absenteeism because of a hangover or intoxication, low productivity due to loss of motivation, preoccupation at work about using after work, preoccupation after work about problems at work. Consequently, the spouse or caring fellow employee may choose to make excuses for the user so that he will not lose his job. This person is less able to function, *so* people who care about him decide to function more. But he is enabled to function less *because* others have decided to function more.

A Major Difference

There is a difference, however, between a broken leg and chemical dependency. In the case of a broken leg, if those who care become more functional to compensate for my incapacity, eventually my leg will heal. When it does, I will get back on my two feet, go back to work, take out the trash, mow the lawn, go to the elders meeting, and take back any other responsibilities that belonged to me in the first place. That is something to remember about broken legs. If you leave them alone, they go away.

In the case of chemical dependency, when those who care compensate for lack of function on the part of the dependent person, the chemical dependency *will* progress. The person *will* be able to continue being dysfunctional. That is something to remember about chemical dependency. If you leave it alone, it gets worse.

All of this results from negotiating away reality, with good intentions. Loved ones believe that all of the compromising will help the dependent person. The compromise, however, cannot possibly help. The efforts of family members to alleviate family dysfunction actually perpetuate the cause of the dysfunction in the first place. The second consequence of system dysfunction, then, is that members of the family become functionally reactive.

It Gets Worse!

As the process continues, even the relationships of family members with those members *other* than the dependent person are affected. This happens because relationships as well as individuals are preoccupied with the person in the center of the family's focus. Although such things are rarely said out loud, relationships between family members are preoccupied with questions such as:

- What can we say to help so-and-so?
- What should we avoid saying so he will not get angry, sad, hurt, or drunk?
- What should we avoid saying so we do not get hurt?
- What should we do to help?
- What should we make sure not to do?
- Who can we get him to talk to?
- Who can we get to talk to him?
- What can we get him to read?
- How can we get him to church, summer camp, or work?

It is very common for members of such a family to focus so much on their relationship with the dependent person that they neglect their relationships with each other. As a parent, I have many relationship hats to wear. I have to be dad, friend, companion, and teacher to my children. I have to be husband, lover, friend, companion, and support to my wife. I have to be friend, employee, employer, fellow member of the body of Christ, counselor, and teacher to those outside my family. In addition, I have to keep the hats straight and wear each one when it is appropriate.

In a family where there is a chemically dependent person, family members tend to wear those hats that apply exclusively to their relationship with the dependent person. If one of the children has the problem, there always seems to be one crisis or another. Dad seems constantly to have to wear his "Dad" hat with regard to this child. Therefore, his hats with regard to his other family members are left on the shelf, and those relationships suffer. Eventually, he may realize that he is powerless to fix his dependent child, but by that time his relationships with other family members may be damaged.

Each person in the family, as well as each relationship, is focused on the problem person. Everyone in the family revolves around the member whose life revolves around chemicals.

When the Dependent Person Leaves

Suppose the chemically dependent person leaves the role as the focal point of the family. He might get drunk and die in a car accident, or he might run away from home, never to be seen again. A divorce might occur and the dependent person moves away, or he marries and leaves home. Perhaps old age catches up with him.

This is a very serious situation! A long hard road of compromises, adjustments, accommodations, and negotiations has been traveled for this family to survive the pain, dishonesty, and emptiness that are so much of the chemical dependency process. Do you think that simply extracting the chemically dependent person from the middle of the family erases the effects and reverses the process? Do they suddenly acquire new living skills? Do they just return to functioning healthfully as they did before chemical dependency infiltrated their family? The answer to all of these questions is *no*!

This family has been immersed in spiritual, emotional, and psychological chaos. They may have experienced physical effects as well. Sixty perfect of all violent crimes against persons are alcohol-related. Hundreds of thousands of people are affected by the more than twenty-five thousand alcohol-related traffic accidents yearly. Of the reported child abuse cases in my county of residence, 85 percent come from families where there is chemical dependency. The self-esteem of family members and the family as a system has plummeted. The efficiency of the family, both emotionally and functionally, has all but disappeared. Shame, anger, inadequacy, and guilt motivate most of what happens here. If this is a Christian family trying to have a positive self-assessment based upon following God's law, the shame and guilt are probably worse.

Jesus said, "I have come that they may have life, and that they may have it more abundantly" (John 10:10). There is no abundance of life in this family. Survival is the name of the game. Survival skills are what people acquire and use in order to win the game of survival. Survival *could* be considered winning, unless it is compared to abundant life. The absence of the dependent person in the family is not the same as acquisition of healthy living skills and supportive relationships on the part of remaining family members.

When the Dependent Person Gets Well

One instance may occur in which a chemically dependent person ceases to be the focal point of the family—the dependent person begins to recover and regain health. Perhaps through a self-help group, a treatment program, or a spiritual awakening, the person has realized his dilemma and accepted help. When a person who is learning to be functional is put back into the middle of a family that is dysfunctional, a new uncomfortable situation is created. The family does not know how to live with a sober, honest, responsible person. No one knows how to support health, only further dysfunction.

Three things may happen when this occurs. First, the pain and discomfort causes family members to begin a process of recovery themselves. Families usually get better one person at a time. It is difficult for this to happen, however, because of the rigidity and delusion in the family system.

Second, the chemically dependent person comes to the conclusion that it is very unlikely that he will be able to maintain his sobriety and recovery in this dysfunctional environment. He is the only one struggling with healthy issues. If he concludes that the family members simply are not willing to learn how to support health and honesty, he may leave the family. Some people spend years threatening their dependent spouse with divorce if they do not quit drinking. Suddenly one day the dependent spouse does stop, begins to recover, and leaves the family anyway.

Third, the chemically dependent person returns to a family that only knows how to support dysfunction, encounters people who are not willing to learn how to be healthy, and returns to using. As a matter of fact, the family actually *needs* the person to stay dysfunctional in order for it to function as usual. They may consciously or unconsciously sabotage that person's recovery process.

Losing Your Lifelong Vocation

Can you imagine how you would feel or react if you had spent most of your life trying to fix someone else in your family? You focused your time and attention on one member at the expense of others, you compromised and negotiated away your feelings and insights, you manipulated to the point where dishonesty and people-pleasing masqueraded as honesty. And suddenly, that person got better! He became sober and honest. He wanted back all of the responsibilities you had gotten so good at taking on yourself. He no longer wanted you butting into the middle of his relationships with everyone else. You would be relieved, right? Wrong! You would be out of a life-long job, the purpose and focus of your life would be gone, and you would have nothing to do, no one to fix.

Recently I counseled a young woman who was a college student living at home with her mom and dad. She described her family situation and her increasing awareness of her own unhealthy behavior and attitudes. She was suspicious about her father's alcohol consumption. She said that her dad would have fits of anger in which he would say things to and about her that were very hurtful and derogatory. Through all of this, her mom stood by her and seemed to be her only supportive family member. Mom went to great lengths to calm Dad down and to ease my client's hurt feelings. Sometimes this took days or weeks. Eventually Dad would be overcome with guilt for acting so harshly with his daughter and would apologize, and things would be fine—until the next time.

One thing caused my client a great deal of confusion, however. Whenever she and her dad were not getting along, she and her mom were close. But when there was peace with Dad, her mother was antagonistic and surly. It almost seemed that she tried to provoke a conflict between daughter and father.

There is a rather simple explanation for this, once you understand dysfunctional family systems. When daughter and Dad were getting along, Mother was unemployed. She had actually grown to *need* fights between her two loved ones. If there was not a war, she started one.

I have seen people try to get their spouse to go to church every week for years. Spouse No. 1 believes that this will solve whatever problem there is in the relationship. This solution betrays naïveté and self-righteousness on the part of spouse No. 1. And then one day, lo and behold, spouse No. 2 decides to try it. When the intentions are announced, the reply has often been, "Big deal! What's one time going to help?" after which spouse No. 2 decides to stay home. This response sabotages the healthy decision and keeps spouse No. 1 in work.

Sabotaging Recovery with Good Intentions

I once had a teenage client in treatment whose family refused to become involved in the process. This guy was one of the best liars and storytellers I have ever met. He was so charming it was hard to be angry with him even though you knew he was probably lying. His family took a long time to catch on to the fact that he lied more than he told the truth. Once they did, they stopped believing everything he said even if it was true.

In treatment he learned to live without chemical use, and he acquired healthy living skills. He also learned to deal with his past problems and emotions. He learned to be honest and came to believe that being honest with God, himself, and others was extremely necessary if he was to continue to grow.

Since his family was not involved in their own recovery process and had not witnessed his, problems soon developed. Not long after returning home, he took the family car on a date with his girlfriend. He promised to be home at a certain hour. On his way home, the car got a flat tire. It was pouring rain, so he waited a while before attempting to change the tire. When the rain did not let up, he decided to change it anyway, only to discover that there was no lug wrench in the trunk. He remembered seeing a farm two miles back. Through the downpour he trudged in hope of finding a benevolent farmer. Forty-five minutes later he and the farmer arrived on a tractor. He replaced the tire, took his date home, and returned home himself. It was three hours later than the time he had said he would be home.

Both of his parents were awake and furious. They gave him the third degree and accused him of using chemicals again. They were not interested in explanations that sounded to them like pretreatment lies. Their response was, "Sure, we've heard all of this before. You've been using; just admit it." In telling me about this later, he confided, "When I lie they don't believe me, and when I tell the truth they don't believe me. What's the use of going straight anyway?"

Please do not get hung up on the fact that he could have called home. He could have, but that is not the point of sharing the story. The point is to demonstrate that unless family members are involved in their own process of growing healthier, they will continue to function in the way that resulted from accommodating the dysfunction of the dependent person. Not only this, but they will also function in a way that supports the dependent person in staying in or returning to unhealthy behavior patterns.

Do you see any opportunities for ministry yet?

5

Infected for Generations

Individuals go through a process in order to become dependent upon chemicals. We call them *chemically dependent*. Those who love them, who lack awareness, and who have shame go through a process very similar to the chemical dependency process. We call them *codependent*. A codependent is a person who seeks to get his sense of well-being from the dependent loved one.

Beginning the Downward Spiral

First, think back to what chapter 3 says about the chemical dependency process.

Suppose that one day you are hovering around normal, and you notice something negative, an action or attitude, in the life of your chemically dependent loved one. Of course, at this point you probably are not aware of his chemical dependency. Perhaps he lies about something, or the quality of performance in a certain area of his life decreases. How do you feel? You could feel angry, hurt, embarrassed, frustrated, ashamed, confused, any number of feelings.

So there you are carrying a heavy emotion. You now have several options from which to choose. You could make a healthy choice by following up on the heavy emotional signal, go to the other person and confront the situation honestly, indicating what effect his behavior is having upon you. On the other hand, you could excuse the person's behavior in the hope of not feeling what you already feel. You could blame someone or something else for your loved one's action and transfer your feeling toward that other "cause." You will still have the feeling, however. You could quote yourself Bible verses about why you should not feel how you already feel. But this would probably only cause you to feel guilty. You could counterfeit joy and patience, hide behind a smile, and just plain stuff the feeling. Or you could tell other people about what happened (which doesn't help; it only causes sides to form).

Learning to Lie about Feelings

The following illustration demonstrates what happens in chemically dependent families. A little girl spends most of her day drawing and painting a picture for her mom who is at work. Mother comes home forty-five minutes late and is greeted by a dancing, prancing bundle of giggles who thrusts a huge, multi-colored picture in her face. Mother has had a hard day, got stuck in a traffic jam on the way home, and wants to sit down and relax with a drink. She says, "I'll look at the picture later; Mommy's tired." The daughter remains undaunted. "But Mommy," she sings, "this is for you! I worked all day!" At this point, the mother yells back, "*I* worked all day! Get out of here and leave me alone!" She goes to the liquor cabinet, mixes a drink, and retreats to the den. (Note: This happens in many homes where there is no chemical dependency. Taking the chemical out of the picture does not make the effect less devastating.)

How does the daughter feel? Probably sad, frustrated, and rejected, maybe angry. When I have used my own troubles and frustrations as "good enough" reasons to be insensitive and cruel to my children, they have been encouraged to talk to me and tell me the effects that my behavior has had upon them. My response is usually to touch them and thank them for telling me. Then I apologize for dumping my feelings about other things on them. Finally, I either look at the picture or ask for some private time, after which I will look at it. The situation is over, the relationship is restored, and we go on from there.

In the chemically dependent family, such is not the case. If the daughter tried to be honest with her mother, she might be punished or be told, "Don't you *ever* talk to me like that. What kind of daughter talks to her mother like that? I want respect!" If that happens, the little girl will come away from her mother with more heavy emotions than when she went to her.

Not only that, but if she gets punished or shamed enough for trying to be honest with her mother, she may give up trying to be honest at all. She may decide to act like a "nice," polite, quiet, respectful little girl when Mother is around. But while she may learn to pretend that she is emotionally OK, she really still has the heavy emotions.

Trying to Be Real with an Expert Pretender

Now let's try a different slant. This time, instead of going to her mother to work it out, which she has learned is too hurtful, she waits until her father gets home and tells him the whole story. How does Dad feel? Sad, frustrated, angry at Mom? Compassion for the little daughter?

Dad might tell his daughter to confront her mother. He might confront her himself. These alternatives are unlikely, however, because people get hurt for being honest in this home.

Suppose Dad says, "Well, your mother has had a hard day at work. And besides, she's working so you can get that bicycle you want. Try to understand." This tells the daughter that she should not feel the way she already feels. It is also saying that there is a good enough reason for parents to say hurtful, shaming things to their daughters. Dad might even be angry at the little girl himself, for bothering her mother. This blames the daughter for the mother's inappropriate outburst, adding to her heavy emotional state. If Dad yells at Mom, the child may feel guilty for causing a problem between her parents.

And what is Mom doing while the little girl and her father are struggling with discovering ways to stuff their feelings and excuse their loved one's inappropriateness? She is probably working on her second drink, close to being "free" from her own heavy emotions.

It Gets Worse . . .

The process continues. Maybe you are a parent and the chemical user is your daughter. Her grades suddenly dip dramatically. Last year's As and Bs are this year's Cs and Ds. How do you feel? Confused, angry, scared, ashamed?

Who or what is responsible for the change? Does your daughter have a drug or alcohol problem? Never! She's just going through a stage. After all, her older brother went through this when he was this age. It will pass. Perhaps she listens to too much rock music, or maybe it is her friends; they have changed a lot in the last year.

Ask your daughter. Well, she says she is bored with life and her teachers are all jerks this year. Do you believe her? After all, it *is* easier to have a daughter who is going through a stage, hooked on rock music, bored with life, whose teachers are jerks, than one who is on alcohol or drugs, isn't it?

86

And Worse . . .

The process continues. Perhaps your mother is so strung out on alcohol or prescription medication that you are afraid to have friends come over to visit. They might see how unmanageable the house has become. They might hear the ranting and raving over even the smallest things. Then one day your friend says, "Hey, let's go to your place and listen to music. We haven't been there for a while." How do you feel? Scared, embarrassed, ashamed? "Oh," you lie, "my little brother has chicken pox." Do you feel guilty for lying? You should, you know. Lying did not come so easy at one time.

"Where is your husband?" asks his boss over the phone. "He's sick today. I'm taking him to the doctor later," you lie. "Daddy, why doesn't Mommy act like she loves us anymore?" ask the children. "She does," you lie. "You're too busy with your friends to notice," you blame. "And don't ever talk that way about your mother again," you explode, even though you have been wondering the same thing. "Why isn't your son in youth group anymore?" asks a fellow church member. "Oh, he's decided to study so he can catch up in school. He's planning to start coming at the beginning of next quarter," you lie. You have not even talked to your son for more than five minutes in the last week.

Becoming Blind to Vital Signs

How do you feel? Guilty? You should, and you should ask for help. But somewhere along the line *you* have changed. You have a lot of "good enough" reasons for lying. And all of them indicate that you believe that you are not responsible. "After all," you reason, "people shouldn't butt in where they aren't welcome." "If the church had been this interested in the first place, this wouldn't have happened." "Those two friends of hers have caused all this," or "The boss is always on his case." "Now we don't want to upset Grandpa and Grandma. Just tell them that Junior didn't come because he had a basketball game." Here is a good one: "We don't need anyone's help or advice. We're a family, and we'll work this out by ourselves."

No you will not! You are deluded, just like your chemically dependent loved one. As a result of having focused on that person and his behavior, you have neglected and damaged other relationships and have isolated yourselves from help. You have excused, ignored, blamed, and explained away what was happening. You have treated others as though they could not handle the truth, when it is you who cannot handle it. You have denied being affected for so long that you are in the same emotional pit as the dependent person, and you did not even have to use chemicals to get there. You cannot tell what is true or false anymore, and you do not know what helps or does not help anymore. You are deluded.

My Most Extreme Case

On one occasion, I was facilitating a group therapy session for both dependent and codependent people. In the group was a married couple, both in their fifties. After attending for a couple of weeks, the husband, who was an alcoholic, decided that he no longer needed to be there. After all, he had been sober for three weeks. This, he believed, would have been impossible if he really were an alcoholic, and he stopped coming. He had adopted a pattern of getting counseling for a while and then quitting. This enabled him both to meet his wife's demands that he get counseling and avoid getting help for his problem.

The wife continued to come. As her discomfort over being there alone and "telling stories" about her husband dissipated, she began to tell the group of her family's twenty-year battle with alcoholism. For the first ten years, her husband's drinking was a concern but certainly nothing about which to panic. The next five years was a time during which he began to spend more evenings drinking away from home, coming home from work late, and neglecting his responsibilities as a husband and a father. Through it all she explained away his behavior, accepted it, justified it, and tolerated it.

The one thing she could not tolerate was that the family's finances were in a shambles. She was given little money to run the household, pay the bills, or buy school supplies, food, or clothing. She was given the message that evidently she was a very poor money manager, so she tried harder. She was also given the message that she was lazy because she did not seek outside employment to supplement the family's inadequate income, so she felt defective.

Through it all, she simply could not make ends meet. Having the lights, heat, or telephone turned off was a frequent occurrence. Finally, one Friday the mortgage company notified her that unless she paid the $1,000 they owed by the following Tuesday, they would lose the house. Well, despite the measly amount of money she had been given over the past five years to operate the family, she had managed to scratch together over $1,000 and had it hidden in jars, socks, cupboards, and drawers throughout the house. The following Tuesday she went down to the mortgage company and paid the bill in cash. She admitted that being able to do this made her feel very important and needed.

The last five years (which brings us up to the group therapy sessions mentioned at the beginning of the illustration) were more of the same, except worse. She got a part-time job to help out the family, which also made her feel important and useful. Despite her efforts to subsidize the family income, the lights and telephone were once again in danger of being switched off, and the mortgage company was making threatening noises as well. She was tired, angry, and bitter.

The group was exceptional with her. They explained how her husband was out of control and pouring down his throat the resources needed to finance the family. She nodded in agreement. They explained how she had begun to believe that she was the cause of the family's financial woes. They told her this was not true, and she cried in relief. They pointed out how she had set out to become the solution, since she believed she was the cause in the first place. She admitted to being tired and angry because it did not work. They showed her how her efforts to rescue the family, even though they felt fulfilling at the time, merely enabled her husband to continue being irresponsible. She had simply prolonged the inevitable. Because of the supplemental income, her husband could continue to drink and squander his income. Again, there was an understanding nod from her.

They said that the reason she felt so tired and angry was that she had sacrificed her own needs, integrity, and relationships with others. She had poured all of her emotions and energy into fixing a situation she did not have the power to fix. They reminded her of her responsibility to herself and to the family, and of the need to learn healthy ways with which to deal with the situation. They suggested that she learn how to expend effort in areas that truly helped, rather than helping the family's problems continue. She thanked them for this permission.

All in all, the session was very enlightening for everyone, and she hugged and thanked us all afterward. But when everyone had left, she crept back in the office with the stealth of a cat burglar, looking over her shoulder to make certain no one from the group had followed. And with her next words, she illuminated my understanding of codependency delusion like nothing before or since. She said, "I know that the group means well. And they are probably right about some things. But tell me, honestly. Don't you think I should go out and get another part-time job?"

Everyone Is His Own Problem

If you are codependent, it is not the fault of the dependent person. You are not in the emotional pit with someone else to blame; you are responsible for your state. You did not ask for help; you made up excuses, lies, and explanations. You neglected your relationships with others because of your preoccupation with the dependent person. You flushed your integrity by supporting on the outside that with which you disagreed in your heart. You neglected your own health to put all your effort into fixing the dependent person, as if your well-being depends upon how he is doing.

And it does, just like his well-being depends upon chemicals. When he looked good, tried harder, made promises, willed himself sober, even lied, you believed him and felt better. You needed and still need him to be healthier than he actually is, so you saw him that way. That is why when he slips back into the pit, thus proving his inability to will himself healthy, you slip back into the pit with him. You are codependent.

Codependency: Serving the Creature Rather Than the Creator

A codependent is a person who is dependent upon the chemically dependent person for his "highs." When the dependent person manages to force himself into temporary improvement, the codependent is high. When the dependent person fails, the codependent is low. And just as the dependent person blames something outside of himself as the cause of his problems, so too does the codependent turn to an outside source for either his well-being or his problems. The codependent blames the chemically dependent loved one.

Actually, I am not particularly fond of the term codependency. First, when I started working with people struggling with addictions, I would not have diagnosed someone as codependent unless somewhere in her life story I found a relationship with a dependent person. Yet what I have observed most often is that the unhealthy relationship skills, the tendency to turn to people and external circumstances to provide acceptance and worth, and the urge to fix other people are brought into relationships by the codependent person herself. Second, a codependent is an addict even though the term itself seems to connote a second-class dependency.

Remember the discussion about idolatry in chapter 1? Codependency is an addiction that results from an idolatrous relationship with someone who is chemically dependent. A codependent person turns to something other than God as his source of well-being. If another human being is your false god, you do not want a broken god who is drunk, irresponsible, and causes embarrassment. You want a sober and responsible god, one that will cause you to feel proud. Therefore, you must fix your god, which is why so much time and energy, his own and other people's, is spent by the codependent trying to fix the chemically dependent person. That is also why it is so difficult for the codependent to let go, even though the efforts are proving to be useless.

Very often I see this person in my office. He or she tells me all of the horror stories about his or her family and the behavior of the chemically dependent loved one. Next comes the boast about "just trusting the Lord to solve everything. Everything is in His hands and I'm just going to wait faithfully." It just is not true in most cases. "God" for the codependent person is one of two people.

First, "God" is the dependent loved one who is the focus for the codependent's security, peace, and happiness.

Second, "God" is the codependent person himself. At the same time he is "trusting God," *he* is doing all of the work. He is making telephone calls, dropping hints, leaving literature in conspicuous places, pouring the spouse's booze down the drain, checking up on every move made, giving advice to everyone concerning how to act around the dependent person, getting advice from everyone concerning everything but chemical dependency, and keeping track of everything being done for which the dependent person should somehow be grateful.

Instead of nurturing growth and dependence upon God only as the source of well-being, the focus of the family becomes one of survival. Therefore, the family has reacted psycho-emotionally and functionally, as described in the last chapter.

Stuck in Survival

There are numerous codependent manifestations of these reactions, all designed to enable family members to survive. For instance, during this process the family needs a person (or people) to over-function in order to compensate for its dysfunction. Whenever the chemically dependent person falls short, this compensating person is there to pick up the pieces. Whenever there is inappropriate behavior, this person has a ready excuse. Every time there is trouble in the relationships between the dependent person and other family members, this rescuer steps in and mediates so that people will get along. He filters out as much sadness and pain for others as he can, even if he has to martyr his own feelings and needs. He is super-concerned, too, about people's issues outside of the family. If you ask how things are at home, he smiles and says, "Fine."

He knows just how to manipulate people to feel or act certain ways, always managing to maintain a righteous, humble manner. He criticizes others until someone else joins in, then quickly transforms into the defender of the accused. And *nothing* he does helps the situation. Deep inside he is angry and bitter, and he probably has stress-related problems, maybe even a little tranquilizer use. He is tired, but never free to rest from his unhelpful, and sometimes unwelcome, helping.

This family also needs someone about whom to feel proud, a performer whose accomplishments represent an island of success in the sea of family failure. This is the person who does it right, is recognized at school, at work, on the playing field, and in the youth group. If money is the biggest measure of success, he sets out to get it. If a degree provides worth, he sets out to earn it. Yet nothing he does helps the situation. So in the midst of all of his external adequacy, he feels inadequate, a good candidate for burnout or an ulcer. He is tired, but never free to rest from achieving.

Very often families like this have another type of person. This is the person who is compared to the performer, followed by the indictment "Not good enough." Where there is conditional love, some people try harder, but this person gives up. He cannot get noticed by achieving, so he fails. She runs away, gets pregnant, achieves poor grades, continually loses jobs. The problem behavior actually provides a welcome refocus of family attention off its issues and onto an individual. He becomes the sacrificial lamb that receives all of the attention and help the family needs. But nothing helps the situation.

She feels hurt and rejected. She is tired, but never free to rest from rebelling.

In addition, this family has become a heavy environment in which to live. They need someone or something else to lighten up things, a jester to provide laughter in the midst of sadness. This is the family "aspirin," the pain reliever who eradicates tension with humor here and cuteness there. Always witty and jokingly critical of the seriousness of others, this impish individual is often the life of the party. He might even try chemicals to heighten the fun. But nothing helps the situation. He feels insecure. He is tired, but never free to rest from clowning.

People pursue different courses to survive pain and erase shame. Some read, paint, watch television, or play video games. Others withdraw into depression or even schizophrenia; still others decide to use chemicals. People who are codependent are high-risk candidates to have a problem with chemicals later.

A Deadly Seed Planted

I hope that you will come away from chapters 4 and 5 with at least two realizations. First, in a family where there is chemical dependency, family members have incredible amounts of pain. At the same time, they often lack the skills and support to deal with the pain. Escape and denial have been presented as the models for handling painful reality. Family members have been taught reliance upon externals that have no power to cause well-being. The likelihood is extremely high for them to become involved with a harmful dependency of their own in the future.

Second, and perhaps worse, is the fact that these family members, in their effort to survive, have learned to accommodate the presence of extremely unhealthy behavior, attitudes, and relationships. Unless they receive help, they will take these skills and tendencies into future relationships, thus setting the stage for devastating problems in relationships not yet formed. Like a double-edged sword, chemical dependency and codependency have the potential to maim and kill relationships for generations.

6

Shame: The Hurt That Keeps On Hurting

Shame is a cancer of the heart and of the mind that relentlessly and unmercifully tears away at people and destroys their relationships. Shame provides the fuel for a host of problems that sap the life out of individuals and their families for generations.

There are four specific reasons why I have included a chapter on shame in a book about chemical dependency. First, if there is chemical dependency in a family, shame is also there buried inside the chemically dependent individual and often other family members as well. Second, many families and churches use forms of shame to try to motivate acceptable behavior. Utilizing shame to attempt to prevent alcohol and drug problems, or any behavior, is utterly antagonistic to the gospel. Third, all too often the only concern of families and churches is to bring chemically dependent people to the point of abstinence. This neglects to confront the shame in the individual and family, thus allowing the soil in which chemical dependency grows to remain fertile. And fourth, shame, as well as strength, fullness, and health, passes from one generation to the next.

Reviewing Our Needs

I have previously stated that human beings have three basic needs. First, we need to be convinced that we are loved and accepted, without strings. In order to get love and acceptance, we do not have to act or refrain from acting a certain way, perform, excel, be polite, or quote Bible verses. And love is not withdrawn because of lack of performance. This love and acceptance come in gift form only, determined by the fullness of the one giving it, not by the actions of the recipient. This love builds people up, because people, not behaviors, are loved.

Second, we need to be convinced that we are capable, valuable, important, special, and worthy. In spite of the fact that some theologians have problems with these qualities ("Secular humanism!" they say), there are biblical terms that communicate the same concepts: *chosen, gifted, called for a purpose, given to one another* (see chapter 12).

I strongly disagree with those who say you have to hate yourself in order to love God. The only passages in the Bible that come close to this kind of idea are those such as Matthew 10:32 and following. However, this passage does not extol self-hate or the hate of others. Rather, it teaches that we must confess Christ before men. In fact, in Matthew 22:37–39, Jesus described the foundation upon which depend the law and the prophets. We are to love God with everything there is about us and love our neighbor as we love ourselves. Unfortunately, many Christians *do* love their neighbors as they love themselves; they hate themselves and pass that hate onto others.

Humility does not equal denying who we are, pushing away what we have been given, and saying we do not count. Humility involves lifting others above ourselves instead of asserting ourselves over them. As a result of knowing who we are and what is ours, we can be givers and not takers. Jesus' frame of mind in John 13 when he washed the disciples' feet is described in verse 3 as "knowing that the Father had given all things into His hands, and that He had come from God and was going to God." It is impossible to give away something we do not have.

Third, we need to be convinced that we are not alone. There are two aspects to this. We need to know that we are not the only ones who think, act, feel, and struggle as we do. Many times clients tell me about something with which they are struggling and then look to see my response. Not only do I surprise them by *not* falling off the chair, but most often I am able to tell them that I know of someone who is struggling with exactly the same issue. I cannot count the times clients have cried or laughed or emitted audible sighs at the relief of discovering that they are not some special case in the universe. We also must know that there are resources and support in times of need. We are not alone!

The Bible declares that God has already acted to meet these needs in Christ. And Philippians 4:19 affirms that He will continue to do so. "And my God shall supply all your need according to His riches in glory by Christ Jesus." As those in relationship with Christ, God loves, calls, and seals us. He forgives, chooses, frees, and cleanses us. He calls us for a purpose and gifts us to accomplish it. We used to be far away, but He has brought us near. We used to be His enemies, but He has made us His friends, His children. He will never leave us nor forsake us. Our relational support does not stop with Christ. The New Testament describes further support with concepts such as "fellowship" and the "body of Christ."

Misunderstanding Our Purpose

I believe that the primary purpose of families and churches is to convince their members of these things. Cementing the gospel in our members is the main job that faces us, not motivating appropriate godly behavior with external pressure. Ample biblical evidence indicates that there *will* be obedience and service in those who understand, believe, and accept their gifted identity and resources. In Matthew 7:17, Jesus says, "Even so, every good tree bears good fruit, but a bad tree bears bad fruit." He is simply stating a fact, a diagnostic test that allows one to know if the tree is good or bad. Jesus is not pep-talking bad trees to bear good fruit. Similar verses that contain statements and not "shoulds" are John 14:15, 15:5, and 1 John 2:3–4.

Notice that these verses do not try to motivate certain behavior. They are simply statements of the fact that obedience and service are natural consequences of faith in Christ. They suggest that the reason there is no life on the outside is that there is no life on the inside. If there is no fruit, there is no life. The tree that was chopped down in Matthew 7:19 was chopped down because it was a bad tree, not because it did not produce good fruit.

We have even relegated James 2:14–17 to a "should" passage, when it is really an incredible barometer of the heart. In verse 14, James asks the rhetorical question: "What does it profit, my brethren, if someone says he has faith but does not have works? Can faith save him?" The same question is raised in verses 15 and 16 with a hypothetical situation. He then answers the question in verse 17, "Thus also faith by itself, if it does not have works, is dead," and again in verse 20. These are statements, not shoulds.

Remember our discussion of life and death in chapter 1? Death is where there is no life. And dead faith is where there is no faith. The reason faith without works cannot save anyone is that it is faith that is dead, and therefore absent. The absence of works is not something that James is using to motivate works.

He is saying that it indicates the absence of faith. Dead faith is the same as no faith at all, and thus cannot save.

Unfortunately, many families and churches never raise heart issues at all. They are preoccupied with works. Instead of affirming each other in who they are and what they have in Christ, they affirm one another for what they do. Not only does this fail to build people (behavior is being supported, not people), but it is especially damaging to new Christians who still tend to think about themselves as they used to because they put confidence in the flesh. It results in their obeying and serving out of a sense of guilt and duty, and seeking to earn God's favor with positive behavior done in His name.

The Danger of Paying for the Gift

A very dangerous manifestation of affirming people based on positive behavior in the name of God is the suggestion that people need to pay God back for what He has done for them. This is the mentality I call "Charge-Your-Salvation." I wonder, is it possible to pay for salvation on the installment plan? Never! Let's say my refrigerator breaks and I need to purchase a new one. I go to the store and tell the clerk, "I want that one." He says, "Fine, that will be $500, please." I give him the money, take the refrigerator, and go home. I now have a refrigerator for which I paid. It was not a gift. But what if I had said, "I don't have $500," when the clerk asked for the money? He probably would have said, "That's OK. You can give us $25 a month for the next twenty months and take the refrigerator now." That's great! I still get my refrigerator, but it is still not a gift. I am just paying for it after I get it. The Bible says that life, value, and meaning are gifts. Charged salvation is not salvation at all.

The degree to which people are filled with the fact that they are loved and accepted without strings, that they are capable and valuable and not alone, is the same degree to which they will love, serve, and build others out of fullness and freedom. The degree to which they do not know these things is the same degree to which they function out of obligation and shame. If you are to grasp fully the concept of shame and the ways in which it affects and controls people's lives, it is essential to remember the difference between a gift-based identity and a performance-based identity.

Guilt: A Valuable Signal

At this point, understanding the difference between guilt and shame is important. Guilt is both an emotion and a status. When I act in a way that is inconsistent with who I am or violates a standard I hold to be right and true, I feel guilty. Guilt is the feeling of having done something wrong. I *should* feel guilty when I do something wrong. Guilt is there to tell me about my behavior, to motivate me to do what I must to return to the limits of my identity and values.

Outside of a relationship with Christ, an individual is a guilty person. This is the status of guilt. God's standard is so high that it is impossible for anyone to meet it with performance. As a matter of fact, the Law was given for the very purpose of convincing people to abandon performance-based acceptance by God and accept His love based on His Son's performance. "All have sinned and fall short of the glory of God," asserts Romans 3:23. They are guilty. This comes closest to the meaning of shame, which will be discussed shortly.

Outside of a relationship with Christ I am a guilty person, whether I *feel* guilty or not. Nothing or no one but God can change that. Suppose that Fred is guilty of committing a crime and goes to court. After a lengthy trial and much deliberation on the part of the jury, the verdict comes back "not guilty." The fact that the court found Fred not guilty does not mean he is not guilty. He *is* guilty. The court has not erased his guilt, because the court is not able. In fact, in Fred's case, the court has even failed to perceive his guilt. My guilty status is up to Christ, and only He can do anything about that. If I am in relationship with Him, He has already done it. "There is therefore now no condemnation to those who are in Christ Jesus" (Rom. 8:1).

That leaves us to do something about our emotion of guilt. Guilt is a good learning tool if we recognize and heed it. Ignoring guilt will cause problems in the outside systems of which we are a part and in the inside systems that are a part of us. Since the feeling of guilt is about what we *do*, we can do something about it. If we do something and feel guilty, our responsibility is to make amends, confess the wrongdoing, and come back within our boundaries. If we take the appropriate steps to change the situation or restore the relationship, the feeling of guilt *will* go away. Guilt will have served its purpose. God built us that way.

Shame: The Indictment That Feeds on Itself

However, if the guilt does not go away, it is shame, and it did not go away because shame is not about behavior. Shame is about *you*, not about what you *do*. Shame is the painful feeling of being bad as a person, a sense of being seen in a diminished, devaluated way, and it tells you that you are deficient, inadequate, and unworthy. Something is wrong with you. You are lacking, empty, and defective. Shame equals self-rejection. Shame is not a feeling; it is a perception or mindset.

103

I can tell that a person has shame when he says things like "I am so ashamed," "Dumb old me," "I can't believe I'm so stupid," "What's the matter with me?" "It doesn't matter what I think (feel, need)," and "I don't fit." Words such as *tired*, *empty*, *useless*, and *meaningless* betray the presence of shame.

The fact that man lost life in the Garden of Eden establishes our defectiveness. The impossibility of acquiring life and earning God's approval through performance, as demonstrated by the Law, means that we are defective in our ability to change our defectiveness. Society, families, and even churches are places where shame, not love and acceptance, is cemented.

Cementing Shame

In our culture we are concerned with speed, efficiency, and quantity. Those who are slow, disorganized, or even methodical and artistic are indicted. We are preoccupied with beauty, which shames those who are unattractive, or even plain by that standard. Our focus on youth shames those who are older. The fact that we are a society consumed by sexuality shames flat-chested females and males who lack that "animal quality." People who struggle with their weight are told they are defective by the never-ending wave of gimmicks to make them thin. Our focus on material possessions, power, and status shames the poor, the weak, and even those who choose to live simply.

Shame is reinforced in families as well. Comparing two children shames one. The one being compared gets the message that he would be more acceptable if he were more like the other. Obviously, putting people down with names shames them. When a little boy cries, we shame him by telling him not to be a baby. When a little girl gets angry, we shame her by telling her to be a nice little girl "or don't come out of your room until you can." This says, "We don't care how you really feel on the inside. Look good on the outside." When our child spills his milk, we say, "What's the matter with you? You're so clumsy." This is not about milk, or even spilling it; it is about the child. And what about the always popular "Shame on *you*," or "*You* should be ashamed," or "Have *you* no shame?"

Neglect (failing to meet needs when present or not being present at all) says, "You are not important enough for me to be here for you." Families have been given to people to meet needs. Abuse is anything anyone does to cause by force the performance of those who are less powerful or who see themselves as less powerful than the perpetrator of the abuse. Abuse shames because it says, "Perform or get hurt." Physical abuse is possible because of the strength, loudness, quickness, or other form of power on the part of the abuser. Physical abuse affirms the lack of specialness and power on the part of the victim. Sexual abuse says to the victim, "You are here to meet my needs. What you think or feel does not matter. Your wants and needs do not count."

When abuse happens with the threat to "keep quiet or else," the shame is doubled. The message is, "What I am doing to you is a bad thing (thus, the need to keep it quiet). And you are so worthless that I can do this bad thing to you and get away with it." What a hopeless feeling to have someone stealing your worth and be (or at least, feel) powerless to do something about it. How lonely for a person to love someone who is having a love affair with alcohol or drugs. Even when they are around, they are not around. How horrifying for an abused child to have her tiny doll cut to shreds with the abuser's threat that if she tells, the same thing will happen to her. How overwhelming for sexually molested children to be told they will ruin their parents' marriage if they tell the other parent of the abuse. What a burden for the child to try and protect, with the silence about his pain, a relationship between his parents that does not exist. Shame runs deep in abusive families.

When a family member commits suicide, the entire family is shamed. Suicide insinuates failure, communicates distrust, and cements helplessness. This desperate act says, "I don't even care enough for you to stay around. I reject you and anything you could do or say."

One of the primary purposes of a church is to strengthen people in grace. Yet often churches shame people instead. The shame affirmed by losing the Bible memorization contest in the midweek club far outweighs the benefits of memorizing the verses. We emphasize conforming, quietness, and order at the expense of uniqueness and gifts. Formula books and seminars on how to live the Christian life indict lack of performance and label people as undisciplined or uncommitted. Lawful families and churches shame people by saying, for God, that God is displeased with them because of their lack of lawful behavior.

The Futility of Doing to Be

Ever since the Garden of Eden, man has attempted to eradicate his defectiveness by pursuing inadequate courses. Societal manifestations of this quest are uncountable. All result in further shame and lower self-assessment. Workaholism is the result of the attempt to acquire power, status, or esteem through a job. The workaholic pays dearly and never succeeds in eradicating the feeling of being inadequate. Violence asserts power over someone else, vents heavy feelings, and punishes another for the pain inside. Chemical dependency results from seeking fullness from chemicals and/or attempting to numb shameful feelings altogether. It results in further damage to self-worth.

Family members try to buffer themselves against their shame by being perfect. Some get straight As, join clubs, win

106

scholarships to college, earn educational degrees, or establish thriving practices. All are inadequate means to counteract the feeling of shame and raise the family's self-worth. Others, realizing that they can never measure up, give up. In an attempt to keep the shaming finger pointed in a different direction, some blame others and never admit mistakes or apologize. Others always apologize for everything.

At the present time, I am counseling a woman who is enrolled at a Bible college. She is trying to come to grips with the effects of having grown up in a shaming family system. Another woman, who was my client's childhood friend, is enrolled at the college. One day, my client asked her friend if she could remember anything about visiting her house as a child. The friend replied, "The thing I remember most is that everyone was always saying, 'I'm sorry.'"

Imposing standards of perfection upon self and others seeks relief from shame by means of order and performance. Perfectionism is like a poison ivy rash. The more it itches, the more you scratch it. And the more you scratch it, the more it itches. Judgmentalism results from seeking to gain self-esteem by finding fault in others. When a person's self-esteem shrinks and then finally disappears totally, the person actually disappears himself. We call this suicide.

In churches we turn to the performance of lists of Christian dos and don'ts as the source of our self-assessment. Human beings like lists to which we can compare ourselves. We want to know if we are doing OK.

Trying to Beat the Law

Comparing ourselves and others to the law of God as a measure of our success or victory has three equally unhealthy results. First, a person might experience additional shame because of his lack of performance, which leads to tiredness, lack of creativity, a sense of spiritual dryness, and even disillusionment with God. Why so many people have such a bad taste about churches is not a mystery to me. Church for them represents a place where they are more defective than anywhere else. You can always get persons in this condition to teach, give, or play the organ because they never feel as though they have done enough.

Second, the result may be a person who is self-righteous, which comes from perceived value in God's eyes from living up to the standard. Since self-assessment is based on whether you have done enough, this person *has* to know what is enough. Positive self-assessment results from having done enough. This person is the one that you cannot get to do *anything* more in church because he knows he has already done enough, and chances are he also knows who has not and will encourage you to approach that person. Luke 18:9–14 is Jesus' gift to these people. This Scripture is a parable about a Pharisee and a tax collector who both showed up at the temple at the same time. The Pharisee thanked God that he was OK based upon his superiority in keeping the Law. But the tax collector cried out (v. 13), "God be merciful to me a sinner!" And Jesus said, "I tell you, this man went down to his house justified rather than the other" (v. 14). Beware, those of us whose self-assessment is based on our performance of spiritual dos and don'ts.

Finally, the third result might be a person who is paralyzed. Since mistakes are perceived as having the power to devaluate, and the environment only accepts on the basis of positive performance, this person will not perform at all. He is the person who does not know his spiritual gifts. He is afraid to try for fear of being ashamed. Shame rejects, blocks learning, and discourages the risk-taking that is necessary for growth.

How the Cancer Spreads

Let me explain how shame passes down. Think of an empty circle that represents every human being. The circle represents the void that yearns for love, acceptance, value, meaning, purpose in life—indeed, life itself. Much has been said already concerning the ways that people try to fill the circle. Life cannot be earned, bought, or discovered. Performance cannot cause life, whether it is negative or gets you elected to the Evangelical Hall of Fame. Life can only be received as a gift because of Christ's performance.

A chemically dependent family, and a lot of "healthy" families as well, cannot be a channel through which God cements the gospel and brings healing, because the members are involved with one form of idolatry or another. Therefore, the family cements shame and causes the members to resort to trying to earn their worth. Since love and acceptance are conditional, based upon performance, people learn to look full on the outside. Expecting people to try to fill themselves teaches them that they were empty before they started.

However, affirmation for performance never builds the person because it is not about the person, it is about behavior. Plus, if the family really is a shame family, it has no fullness from which to affirm one another. You cannot give away what you do not have, which means that strings must be attached to any and all acts of love and kindness. In fact, everything that looks like giving is really taking, which contributes to everyone's sense of emptiness. This family actually devours itself.

On the inside, you will more than likely feel shame if you have come from a family such as that. You probably also have a sense of being defective, unlovable, and undeserving of kindness. In addition, you feel as though you can never do enough, as though you are responsible when something goes wrong (even though you cannot quite figure out how), and as though your job is to meet everyone's needs and keep them happy. You are also probably very tired.

But on the outside, since love and acceptance have depended upon your performance, you have learned to perform, be all things to all people, avoid making waves, and look loving and giving (being careful not to give out too much on one hand, or being taken advantage of on the other). You also support things on the outside with which you disagree on the inside, *or* you assume that you are automatically wrong and that your ability to perceive things correctly is defective.

You probably have a hard time receiving gifts and kindnesses from others. You feel embarrassed and undeserving and will eventually try to reciprocate. Free gifts and unconditional love remind you of your shame. *If they really knew what I was like, they wouldn't be so kind,* you think. *They're just being polite,* you think. And then you say, "Oh, you shouldn't have," politely, and begin hatching your plot to pay them back.

Maybe you have had a relationship with a person who has a lot of shame. This is the person who gives and gives and gives and does not want any credit, until one day he asks you to give or help and you refuse or are not able. Then he says, "After all I've done for you, and I ask this one little thing." That is when you find out that there were strings all along. You may not have been aware of them, but probably you were. Strings have a certain feel about them.

The person who has shame tells you all of her troubles. When you feel compassion and reach out to help, she jerks back and says, "Now, now, it's nothing. I don't want you to worry. Besides, lots of people have it worse than I do. The Lord will work things out." You feel ripped off or bruised, and after enough of this, you begin to feel worn out in this relationship. Maybe you begin to avoid her. Maybe you even lie about why because you don't want to hurt her feelings.

The Marriage "Made in Heaven"

This person comes out of her family looking for someone to rescue her from her emptiness. She (or he) yearns for a hero on a white stallion to meet her previously unmet needs. Very often she finds another person with shame on the inside and fullness on the outside, just like herself, because she learned in her family that how things look is what matters, not what is real. Her emptiness sees his fullness, and his emptiness sees her fullness. Their marriage is "made in heaven."

Each will try to be the perfect spouse (friend, steady date, fellow Christian) for the other person. Each will perform the way the seminars say good husbands and wives should. But all of the giving and loving really has strings attached. The problem is that empty people cannot fill empty people; they can just look like they can. In reality, each person's well-being depends upon the performance of the other. Therefore, neither is free to make a mistake. Sooner or later the partners begin to feel the weight of being the source of each other's well-being. They also are again reminded from inside of their inadequacy to do enough. The relationship is failing. The message? Shame on you!

They give up and get divorced, which cements the shame and proves everything they have always felt about themselves. They are inadequate. Their Christian parents and friends cannot figure out how this happened. She had been president of the church youth group, and he had once considered going into the ministry. The message? Shame on you.

Or maybe they do not give up. Maybe they try harder to fill and be filled by each other. This does not work because empty people cannot fill each other. The message? Shame on you. Well, the Bible says do not get divorced, so they have not. They pat themselves on the back for doing "what God wants." Something I never tell people is to get divorced.

Something I always tell people is that God hates divorce and lousy marriages with equal intensity. People will settle for unhealthy marriages to avoid the shame of divorce, never aware of the web of shame in which they are trapped within the relationship.

It's a Bird, It's a Plane, It's Superbaby!

Have you noticed that the shame of the family of origin has now passed to another generation? Let's go further. Very often this family has a child—sometimes they do so intentionally to try to fix the marriage. At this point the baby is already carrying the responsibility of the success of his parents' marriage, and he is not even born yet. Maybe the parents want a baby so they can give it what they never got. Did you hear it? You cannot give what you never got.

This child becomes the focus of the family. How their child behaves and eventually turns out becomes the last-ditch effort on the part of the parents to erase the shame cemented by *their* parents and the failure of the marriage. Therefore, the child has to perform, do tricks, obey, be cute, quote Bible verses, never spill his milk, and *never* run in church, for the parents to know they are good parents. The needs of the child go unnoticed and unmet. The child grows up empty. But since this is another "law family" that loves and accepts based on performance, the child learns to look full.

In a healthy family, parents are there to be resources through whom God fills the children. In the shame family, children are there to be the sources from whom parents attempt to fill themselves. Since the children are responsible for generating the worth of the parents, they have a lot of power. The day the children realize the power they have is the day they begin to shame their parents with their behavior, *intentionally*.

112

The Great Escape

The children in this family are anxious to leave. There are many ways to do so. They can get pregnant as teenagers and have to leave, find someone to marry as soon as they can, run away, bury their heads in books or between stereo headphones, spend hours and hours watching television, or get drunk or stoned. These last few examples represent ways in which they can stay and leave both at the same time. No matter how they leave, they are searching for something or someone who will erase their shame (a spouse or children, maybe?). And the system passes on again.

The shameful family system tends to perpetuate itself at the expense of its members. The lawful structure that exists actually hides the shame by encouraging family members to sacrifice what is true for the sake of how things look. A "don't talk" rule develops in which people cannot find out what is real. What is real reminds people of their shame; therefore, what is real must be hidden. How things look is what matters, after all. Questions about real things bang against people's shame. It is better to be seen and not heard, after all. Questions must be stopped.

"What's Wrong with You?"

Here are some examples of how this works:

- Child says, "I want to wear the red dress." Parent says, "Oh, you like the blue one better. Besides, the red one makes you look fat."
- Little boy cries. Parents say, "Grow up and don't be such a baby."

- Child asks, "Mommy and Daddy, why are you arguing?" Parent says, "We're not arguing, we're having a discussion. Besides, keep your nose out of where it doesn't belong!"

- Child says, "I'm sad." Parent replies, "Oh, you are too sensitive. I don't know what you have to be sad about. I grew up in the Depression. If you want to see sad, *that's* sad."

- Child screams, "I'm angry!" Parent screams back, "Don't you *ever* talk to me like that again."

- Parent simultaneously spanks and instructs child, each word matching each hit, "Don't-hit-your-sis-ter!"

The messages communicated through this are: you are not capable of knowing what you like, how you feel does not matter, how things look is what matters, your opinions and perceptions are not welcome in this family, do not ask questions, you cannot depend on getting a straight answer, children are less important than adults, you cannot be honest without getting hurt, and do not notice things. In short, *Shame on you, you are defective.*

Shame is also cemented in family members when you answer questions or talk for them, even though they are there to speak for themselves. Shame is cemented with double standards, such as, "Always be honest," and "If that phone call is for me, tell them I'm not here." There is no way for the person to make a choice that pleases.

The Shameful Conclusion

I hope you understand several things after reading this chapter. Let me list them.

1. Getting people to stop using chemicals as the solution to their and your problems is not enough. Behavior, no matter how positive, cannot cause fullness and health.

2. Making an impact on the chemically dependent person is not enough. An impact must be made upon the entire shame-based family system. Otherwise, the system still passes down, even though the harmful dependency is not noticeable. A job, position, or even ministry that keeps you away from your family, even for the reason of providing for them what your alcoholic father neglected to provide for you, perpetuates the shame of your father.

3. The fact that a person has behavior that looks loving, giving, and serving does not necessarily mean that he is a healthy person.

4. A chemically dependent system is not necessary for shame to be present. A system where performance earns value instead of love-confirming value is all it takes to cement shame.

5. Cementing anything other than the gospel of grace taps people's shame and results in additional shame, self-righteousness, or paralysis.

6. Any and all performance, whether it appears positive or negative, that attempts to acquire what Christ earns and God would gladly give is a sin.

7. No amount of right information or singing "Jesus Loves Me" can erase shame. Shame was not cemented by information or songs, but was cemented by law-oriented relationships. Therefore, only "grace-full" relationships with Christ and others bring healing and erase feelings of defectiveness.

PART 2

GOOD NEWS FOR THE CHEMICALLY DEPENDENT AND THOSE WHO LOVE THEM

Introduction

I have spent the greatest part of six chapters describing the nature and processes of becoming chemically dependent and codependent. I have detailed the role played by shame in undergirding and perpetuating unhealthy family systems. The remaining chapters contain principles that are vital to understand before attempting to help chemically dependent people and their family members. In order to have a proper view of helping, one must look at recovery from dependency as a process. I know of no formulas that always help all people get better every time. It is, I believe, a disservice to hurting people to tell them there is a formula that will help them get better.

Programs do not cause growth and health. God does so, through redemptive relationships with Christ and others. These are relationships in which love accepts people where they are, unconditionally. Unfortunately, much Christian counseling and much of what happens in many churches is aimed at getting people to act this way or look that way. Instead of meeting people where they are, listening when they talk about their pain, answering questions that are asked, we often treat people as if we know what they want and need more than they do. As a result, we apply formulas and invent programs to meet those needs. And as I speak in various churches and continue to counsel, I see the results of this kind of help: Christians whose struggles shame them, whose uniqueness embarrasses them, and whose giftedness is circumvented by their efforts to be the perfect Christian, conformed to some religious standard.

A tragedy occurs when chemically dependent people who have had an earth-shattering spiritual awakening try to squeeze everyone else who struggles into their experience. An equal tragedy occurs when those whose recovery is a slower process seek to undermine the validity of the sudden lack of desire for further chemical use in those who have experienced God. How God works, how long He takes, and the methods He uses are His choosing. I suspect Paul was aware of this when he wrote Philippians 1:6: "being confident of this very thing, that He who has begun a good work in you will complete it until the day of Jesus Christ."

I have counseled recovering people, some of whom have experienced instantaneous freedom from their addiction, and some of whom are involved in a process of recovery. My observation has been that more individuals and families fall into the second category. Part 2 of this book is about the process of recovery that can take place within "grace-full" relationships. I do wish, however, to relate some perceptions about many of the instantly cured people I have known. First, while their chemical use and desire to use has been completely obliterated, some of their behaviors and attitudes seem to be unresolved. These simply manifest themselves in ways that are equally damaging but less easily confronted than their chemical use.

Second, many times dependent individuals and family members feel that the end of the chemical use signals the end of the need for help. In this case, abstinence has become another banner of spirituality, a false sense of value equally as inadequate as the use of chemicals.

The reasoning goes something like this. If worth, peace, or security was sought by using chemicals, and it was not found, chemical use was the problem. Therefore, one must do the opposite to find worth, peace, or security; that is, abstain from chemical use. Once that has been accomplished, what else is there to do? The fallacy of this reasoning is the belief that true value can be earned or acquired by behavior.

My intention is not to negate the validity of sudden recoveries. Instead, I offer a word of warning to people who may be unaware of their need to grow, to urge all Christians, dependent or not, to be involved in a growth process, and to confront our attempts to earn value from our own positive behavior.

Quite some time ago, I heard a statistic that has remained with me and has been a great source of comfort to many families with whom I have worked. The statistic states that an average of fifty-four confrontations of his chemical problem are necessary for a dependent person to realize he has a chemical problem. You would think this would be depressing to those who are trying to help a chemically dependent person, but actually it has the potential of being very freeing and encouraging. The statistic means that there is hope, that people eventually realize their need for help. It means that one person does not carry the entire burden of helping someone realize his problem. It means that each individual step or effort is not wasted, even if it appears so at the time.

The fact that the fifty-fourth confrontation has an impact is due to the confrontations preceding it. When a person finally realizes he needs help and seeks it, it will more likely be the result of many things in his life pointing to the problem. Do not give up trying to help just because you do not see results. Do not give up hope!

Ultimately, the purpose of the rest of this book is:

- to set people free to begin their own process of growth and recovery;

- to encourage people to admit their needs and ask for help as they learn that their value as a person is an already-received gift from God through Christ;
- to encourage people to live by faith and not by formula;
- to confront "clone" Christianity, which seeks to unify and offer security based upon sameness on the outside instead of the same Spirit on the inside; and
- to bring good news to the chemically dependent and those who love them.

7

Helping Those Who *Don't* Know
They Need It

Remember the chemical dependency process described in chapter 3? The result of that process is a chemically dependent individual with a god (self, in general, and chemicals, specifically) other than the true God. This person has incredible amounts of denied emotional pain, and he has developed psychological defense mechanisms to convince himself and everyone else that he is fine and something or someone else is the problem. Physically, he may have damaged vital organs.

Five-Step Process to Health

Theoretically, five steps need to be accomplished for the chemically dependent person to be healthy. First, the dependent person must realize the inadequacy of chemical use and the accompanying behavior as a source of value and security. He must come to a point where continuing on his present course becomes more painful than recovering would be. In other words, he must realize that he is chemically dependent.

Second, he must discover a way to get from the spiritual and emotional pit to normal without having to use chemicals to do it. This discovery involves finding a new, more adequate source of well-being. The religious community preaches everything from a relationship with God to self-generated worth in the name of God as the answer to this need. Secular humanism promotes self-generated worth in the name of self and humanity. Alcoholics Anonymous talks about a higher power that can restore us to sanity.

To say that it is not possible for someone to recover from chemical dependency without a relationship with Christ would be incorrect. My opinion, however, is that the only adequate source of life, value, and meaning is a relationship with God through Jesus Christ. Only value and meaning received as a gift because of Christ's sacrifice on the cross can erase the messages of shame so deeply ingrained by our own lack of performance in life and relationships. From the place of Christ-earned value and life, a person can confidently go on to steps three, four, and five. From a place of self-generated worth, a person can proceed only tenuously.

Step three involves thawing frozen, hidden emotional pain and bringing it into the light where healing can take place. This is less likely to happen completely when worth and life depend on personal performance or the benevolence of some nondescript, unknowable force or being. This is most likely to happen in safe, grace-full relationships with God and others.

Fourth, from that same grace-full place, a person can begin to take a serious look at his dishonesty, manipulativeness, and game-playing. These have kept him and others from dealing with the real problem for so long.

Finally, step five involves learning or relearning healthy living skills in order to have a productive life and healthy relationships. This includes learning to go toward people and

God with emotional pain, taking responsibility for actions and decisions, and being unconditionally honest in relationships.

Answering Two Crucial Questions

As we begin to seek ways to help the chemically dependent person proceed through these five steps, asking two important questions is essential. The answers to these questions are the key to whether our help will actually be helpful. First, "Does the person believe he or she has a problem?" All too often, family and church members try to help a loved one through steps two through five when step one has not been realized. Actions speak louder than words at this point, because a person who realizes that he really has a problem will be open to help. On the other hand, a person who does not realize the problem will promise what he has to promise, which is why Jesus had such a ministry to the poor, lame, blind, and sick. They knew they had needs. If a person says he knows he has a problem but does not seek help, chances are he does not believe he has a problem.

Question number two asks, "Has the help being given actually helped?" This question brings me to a simple, yet often missed truth. If a person needs help but does not believe he needs help, the best way to help him is to assist him in realizing his need for help. To put it another way, it is not beneficial to a person who does not know he needs help to treat him as if he knows. This treatment will only result in trying to accomplish steps two through five without first accomplishing step one. This is why, I believe, so much help given by families and the church has not been effective. We have also neglected to assess the effectiveness of the help given.

The first step in helping, therefore, is to ask the two preceding questions. If the person does not know he needs help, and if the help given has not helped, then doing what is necessary to assist that person in realizing his need for help is imperative. The remainder of this chapter will discuss how to and how not to accomplish this. Let me begin with the "how not to's."

Parable of a Helpful Helper

Beginning in Luke 10:25, we find the parable of the good Samaritan. In the parable, we hear Jesus' answer to a lawyer who had rationalized away his own lack of love for his neighbor on the grounds of his ignorance concerning the true identity of his neighbor. The lawyer tried to get out of loving on a technicality. Anyway, we read of the plight of a man on a trip from Jerusalem to Jericho who was robbed, beaten, and left for dead. Upon finding him in this predicament, two representatives of the religious community decided it was not their duty to help and passed by without helping.

> But a certain Samaritan, as he journeyed, came where he was. And when he saw him, he had compassion on him, and went to him and bandaged his wounds, pouring on oil and wine; and he set him on his own animal, brought him to an inn, and took care of him. On the next day, when he departed, he took out two denarii, gave them to the innkeeper, and said to him, "Take care of him; and whatever more you spend, when I come again, I will repay you." (Luke 10:33–35)

Now the point of the parable, I think, is to exhort the lawyer and ourselves to be like the good Samaritan. Being compassionate toward others, going the extra mile, taking care of people in pain, are all admirable behavior. In fact, in verse 37, Jesus said, "Go and do likewise." But let's examine this situation with our two questions and see what happens. The man had fallen into the robbers' hands, was robbed, stripped, beaten, and left half dead. Did he know he had a problem? What a silly question! Of course he knew. Was the help that was given helpful? Again, the answer is yes. The need is understood and the help is helpful.

The "Good Samaritan Syndrome"

But chemically dependent people who have justified their inappropriate use and behavior by blaming others, and who do not know they need help, are looking for Good Samaritans to drag them here, take them there, bail them out, pay the bill, and make excuses for them. When that happens, not only do they not get better, they can actually continue to get worse.

The chances are almost nonexistent that a chemically dependent person will spontaneously realize he has a problem and seek help. This is due to delusion, as well as to the numbing effect of the chemical use that prevents emotional signals and caring confrontations from showing the person that his life has become dysfunctional. Admitting dishonesty and coming to grips with delusion are extremely painful. Admitting and sharing previously buried feelings is extremely painful. Taking personal responsibility for actions and attitudes that have hurt or destroyed relationships is extremely painful. Given a choice, a person is not likely to go toward the pain. Continuing the use of chemicals and staying in delusion and emotional numbness is less painful. For a person to choose the pain of recovery, continuing down the road of dependency has to be more painful.

The problem is that many well-meaning people, in their effort to help the chemically dependent person, actually allow or even help the process to continue. Many times parents or professionals (pastors, teachers, school principals, counselors) get a sense of value from their own performance in their role or from the performance of their children, spouse, or those with whom they work, instead of Christ-earned value received as a gift. When this is the case, they have a lot at stake *not* to see problems, chemical or otherwise.

Personal Rules That Hurt Others

If your rule is "Good parents do not have children who use drugs," then your children could be using and you might not let yourself admit it for a long time. If "Good pastors do not have these kinds of issues in their churches," then the health of individuals and families will be able to disintegrate without so much as a pastoral visit. This applies to "good school principals" and students who use, as well as "good children" with parents who are chemically dependent. This phenomenon *allows* the problem to continue to progress. But trying to help a chemically dependent person without asking the two aforementioned questions creates unhelpful Good Samaritan effects that actually *cause* the process to continue.

Many people are taught that good Christians always protect, always give the benefit of the doubt, always explain, never make waves, always martyr their own feelings and needs, and never feel "bad" emotions. All of this has the effect of preventing the dependent person from experiencing the negative consequences he *should* be experiencing for living the way he is. He is acting inappropriately, and someone else is paying the price. He does not have to be responsible for himself, because someone else is attempting to be responsible for him. The result is that everyone involved becomes irresponsible. The dependent person does not have to be concerned with acting appropriately or making wise choices, because someone is there to excuse, explain away, or bail him out of his unhealthy actions and choices.

How to Help Others Stay Unhealthy

Parents do this in many ways. They blame the teacher or the curriculum when the grades go down. They blame themselves for working too much, working too little, being too strict or not strict enough. They blame the neighborhood or the peers. Parents blame rock and roll (having a son or daughter hooked on rock music is easier to admit than it is to admit that they use drugs). They blame their church. They bribe and plead. They hide their child's behavior from people at church, from relatives, and even from each other. They explain away unhealthy living as a "phase."

Professionals foster the dependency process in many ways also. Pastors shame wives into trying to be submissive enough to fix their alcoholic husbands. They counsel toward a false, self-effort forgiveness that results in temporary, external harmony, but that simply perpetuates the pain. Or they are ignorant of the nature and symptoms of chemical dependency and counsel families for the wrong problems, for years sometimes. Lawyers help people avoid facing the consequences for crimes of which they are guilty. Judges send chemically dependent people to jail without ordering assessments for chemical problems. Social service agencies continue to support families that are not being taken care of by irresponsible dependent people. Counselors continue to offer services to people who continue to use and break commitment after commitment. Doctors treat physical problems caused by chemical use without questioning the dependent person's involvement with chemicals or without asking the codependent where the bruises came from. Or they prescribe mood-altering substance to family members for the stress that results from living in a family where there is chemical dependency.

Spouses foster chemical dependency when they lie to the employer, the kids, or in-laws about their partner's use and behavior, and when they take an extra job to overcome the financial hardship created by their spouse's addiction. They support the addiction when they continue to buy beer for their spouse, all the while lecturing about the evils of drinking, or when they drink with the spouse so they can keep an eye on him or her. They support the addiction when they continue to move the limits they have set concerning how long and how much they will allow themselves and their children to experience the effects of an unhealthy, shame-producing environment.

Remember This!

The important thing to remember is that if chemically dependent persons can continue to live and use chemicals in a way that is harmful to themselves and others, someone is rescuing them from the problems their use *should* be causing them. This is help that is not helpful. In fact, the help offered is more likely really a matter of the helper needing to fix the dependent person in order to fix himself. Or it could be a matter of the helper trying to live up to some performance-based method of earning points with God. In this situation, everything that looks like it is designed to help and fill others is really for the purpose of filling the one who is doing the "helping." It is taking that only looks like giving.

Unfortunately, since many Christians are externally focused and seek abundance from performance of "Christian" formulas, this kind of thing is reinforced. The main goal in helping a chemically dependent person who does not know he needs help is to find ways to assist him in realizing his need.

Sometimes Help Hurts

Some of the "how to's" in helping a chemically dependent person can be easily identified in the following story. In 1979, I was working as a senior counselor in a residential inpatient chemical dependency treatment facility in Minneapolis. At the time I was the primary counselor for twelve people whose ages ranged from fourteen to fifty-five. We met as a group fourteen to eighteen hours a week. I also met with each person individually, as well as with families that were willing to become involved.

One case was a fifteen-year-old boy I will call Rufus. One day during a group therapy session, Rufus got tired of being in treatment, jumped out of his chair, and proclaimed triumphantly, "This place stinks and I'm leaving!" He then stomped defiantly out of the room. He immediately went downstairs to his room, packed his bags, and called his parents, who lived forty-five miles away. He demanded that they come and rescue him from the prison camp treatment center with the mean counselors and other people with problems much worse than his own. This was Rufus's pattern.

His parents' pattern was to feel sorry for him; believe his promises to do better if he could just come home; feel guilty that they had caused him to end up in treatment; find fault with the treatment facility, program, or staff; and come and pick him up. But this time they told Rufus to wait, and they called my secretary who brought a message to me in the group session I was handling. I returned their call and found myself talking to both parents on different extensions. They told me what Rufus had said he wanted and of their frustration with the fact that this kind of thing seemed to be a common occurrence with their son. They were torn.

They said, "We don't know what to do. Rufus wants to leave treatment. He's promised to be good. Should we pick him up, bring him home, and try to make it work?" My answer was in the form of a question. "Do you think Rufus needs to be home with you or here in treatment?" There was a long pause, and finally they each replied, almost in unison, "I think Rufus needs to be there in treatment!" I responded with another question. "If you really believe that Rufus needs to be here in treatment, why would you come and pick him up?" More questions followed. "You would agree that it would be inappropriate for Rufus to rob a bank, wouldn't you?" They agreed. "If Rufus asked you to drive the getaway car, you wouldn't give him a lecture about how bad it is to rob a bank and then drive the car, would you?" They both answered no. I finally said, "Then don't support this action with which you don't agree, either."

This brief interaction between me and these troubled parents offered new parenting options never before considered. For instance, the fact that they did not have to do everything their son demanded had not occurred to them in a long time. The fact had *never* occurred to them that it was dishonest and unhealthy for them, as well as for their son, to support with their behavior what they did not support in their hearts. With a little encouragement on my part, they were able to call Rufus and tell him that they would not help him leave. They said they believed he needed help for his drug problem, and so it would be dishonest and inconsistent for them to take him home again. They were not going to come.

Needless to say, Rufus did not like this at all. He stormed back into the group and sat down. He pouted for a few weeks, and then—he got well! Do you know why? Because he had to. He no longer had parents who would rescue him and bail him out of the consequences of his behavior. They had decided to let Rufus own his dependency and the accompanying problems. They decided to let Rufus be responsible for his own actions and their consequences.

Someone Whose "Yes" Was Yes

My experience as a treatment counselor was full of instances similar to the one with Rufus. I remember a client who entered our facility and made all the commitments in order to do so. In order to be accepted in the program, a client had to agree: to abstain from the use of mood-altering substances while in the program, which included visits to home and friends; to stay as long as we thought necessary and follow our aftercare referral; and to abide by the rules of the facility, for example, complete assignments, be on time, clean their room, and so forth. I do not believe this client was sincere in her promise to keep her commitments. I think she made the commitments because she had to get into a treatment center or the court was going to have her placed in a correctional facility.

One day in the group, six weeks into the program, she said that she realized how dishonest she had been in her life and that she needed to begin clearing the air. Her first major honest announcement was to say that after about a week and a half in the treatment program, she had sneaked out of her room one night and smoked some pot that a friend had smuggled in during visiting hours. I told her that I thought it was great that she had decided to be honest, which seemed like a huge step toward recovery. But I also explained that since she had broken her initial commitment not to use while in the program, I was going to discharge her. I explained that meaning what you say and following through with commitments were important, and that I needed to follow through with my commitment to her by discharging her for using. She was angry, her parents were angry, and her probation officer was angry.

Nevertheless, her parents and probation officer arranged for her to enter yet another treatment center, even though they had threatened that if she did not complete ours, she would serve time in juvenile detention. The same thing happened at that center, so they dragged her to another center, despite similar threats. The same thing happened there.

Then one day, almost a year later, I received a telephone call from the girl. She had turned eighteen and her parents could not make her go anywhere anymore. She had failed enough in life; she had had enough pain to convince her that her chemical use was a problem. She needed help and she knew it. She had remembered one of the few people in her life who had ever meant and followed through with what he said. She wanted to return to treatment and learn to recover. She returned, made and kept her commitments, graduated from the program, and entered a halfway house where she finished school, got a job, and continued her recovery.

Help That Is Helpful

Having illustrated my point ahead of time, I would now like to share some biblical passages that contain important lessons for those who are struggling with knowing how to help. After that, I will continue with principles gleaned from these passages and the previous two illustrations that will serve as a practical starting point from which to decide the best specific ways to help a chemically dependent person (or any person with a problem) who does not know how he needs help.

Let me begin in the book of Matthew, with my comments in parentheses. In Matthew 18:15–17, Jesus said:

> Moreover if your brother sins against you, go and tell him his fault between you and him alone. (*Do not tell his parents, the neighbors, or other Christians. Do not hold a grudge or pretend you have not been affected to show how spiritual you are. Do not counterfeit peace, patience, or forgiveness. Talk directly to the person with the problem behavior.*) If he

hears you, you have gained your brother. (*The relationship is restored, the issue is over.*) But if he will not hear you (*he may be severely deluded*), take with you one or two more, that "by the mouth of two or three witnesses every word may be established." (*What a confrontation this is of so much that goes on in secret, on the telephone, and behind a person's back when people do not like what was said from the pulpit, a decision of the governing board, or the choice made by someone else.*) And if he refuses to hear them, tell it to the church. (*When dealing with a person who is self-deluded, the more pictures of himself he is shown, the greater the chances are that he will see the truth.*) But if he refuses even to hear the church, let him be to you like a heathen and a tax collector (*the final consequences of continuing in inappropriateness*).

Notice that the verse says "let him be," not "make him be." A Jewish person who collected taxes for the Romans was someone who was supposed to be on your side but actually worked for the enemy. A family member, for instance, who is hurtful or abusive is like a first-century tax collector: although he should be for you, he is really against you. Staying away from this person, after all these efforts to confront him, does not make him *be* anything. He acts consistent with how he has already chosen to be, so let him be.

Verse 18 indicates that in the church we do have the power to make things look on earth the way they already look to God. "Assuredly, I say to you, whatever you bind on earth will be bound in heaven" could be translated more accurately from the Greek as whatever you bind on earth *shall have been* bound in heaven (see also John 20:23). The context within which this falls is between the parable of the lost sheep and Jesus' admonition to Peter to forgive his brother on seventy times seven occasions, if necessary. The purpose of the confrontation process and finally the discipline described in Matthew 18:15–18 is one of restoration, not vindictiveness. As someone who fails to recognize his need to change, the person continuing to act inappropriately is rejected. His sin is bound on him, in front of everyone.

In 1 Corinthians 5:1–7, we read of a case of immorality in the life of a man in the fellowship at Corinth. In one of Paul's more scathing confrontations, the apostle reprimanded the church at Corinth for the fact that their arrogance prevented this man from receiving the consequences of sexual immorality. Churches, like families, are systems, and one person's unhealthy behavior negatively affects all (v. 6, "Do you not know that a little leaven leavens the whole lump?"). The Corinthians were urged to remove this person from their midst so that perhaps the painful consequences of that might lead to his salvation (v. 5, "Deliver such a one to Satan for the destruction of the flesh, that his spirit may be saved in the day of the Lord Jesus"). As it was, with the Corinthians ignoring the negative behavior, the man did not need to change. In fact, he probably was unaware that he needed to change.

In 2 Corinthians 7:8–11, Paul talked about a sorrow-producing letter that he had written the Corinthians. Evidently he was glad he wrote it (vv. 8–9, "For even if I made you sorry with my letter, I do not regret it. . . . Now I rejoice"). Paul did not mean that the letter was easy to write or that he liked writing what he did (vv. 8–9, "I did regret it. For I perceive that the same epistle made you sorry. . . . Now I rejoice, not that you were made sorry"). Paul understood that his responsibility was not to shield people from the truth but to tell it, even if it caused sorrow, even to himself. Sorrow that is according to God's will produces repentance (see vv. 9–11).

Luke 15:11–32 contains the parable of the prodigal son. I have added my comments again in parentheses.

A certain man had two sons. And the younger of them said to his father, "Father, give me the portion of goods that falls

136

to me." So he divided to them his livelihood. (*No sermons, no threats on the part of the father. Evidently, the money did rightfully belong to the son.*) And not many days after, the younger son gathered all together, journeyed to a far country, and there wasted his possessions with prodigal living. But when he had spent all, there arose a severe famine in that land, and he began to be in want. Then he went and joined himself to a citizen of that country, and he sent him into his fields to feed swine. And he would gladly have filled his stomach with the pods that the swine ate, and no one gave him anything. (*Did his father not care? Could the father not have sent his son some money or have arranged for his son to have a better job?*) But when he came to himself. . . .

This is as far as I need to go to make the point.

Remember the two questions I shared at the beginning of the chapter? Does the person know he needs help? Is the help being given actually helpful? Let's apply the questions here. Did the prodigal son know he needed help? Not at the beginning, because he was totally unaware of his lack of living skills. The possibility that he would eventually have to fight with pigs for food never occurred to him as he began his adventure. When he found himself working in the pigpen, the answer to question number one became a yes. The main goal of healing him before that time would have been for the father to assist him in seeing his need for help.

Would it have been helpful if the father had begged, explained, rescued, manipulated, or shielded his son from the consequences that accompany the kind of behavior described as "wasted his possessions with prodigal living"? No! Therefore, the father did the most helpful thing he could do. He let his son go and did nothing. Was this helpful? Yes! Does it mean that the father didn't love his son? The rest of the parable shows that he loved him very much. Nevertheless, he had done the hard thing. He let his son go to experience the consequences of his own behavior.

Sometimes God Helps by Letting Go

Two more passages are about letting go, but this time it is God who lets go. Romans 1:18–23 describes people who suppressed the truth, did not honor God, were not thankful, exchanged God's glory, and became fools. Verse 24 says, "Therefore God also gave them up." In verse 25, Paul said they "worshiped and served the creature rather than the Creator," and in verse 26, "God gave them up." In verse 28, we read that "even as they did not like to retain God in their knowledge, God gave them over."

Why does God give people up? Does it mean that He gives up on them? That is what I was taught while growing up. If a person does the things described in Romans 1:18–32, God will give up on them; so watch out, because when God gives up on you, you are given up indeed! However, this is not the reason God gives people up. There is another reason indicated by Romans 3:24ff. Isaiah 5–7 also demonstrates what that reason is.

Isaiah 5 begins with the parable of a vineyard that the keeper planted on a fertile hill so it would have good soil and lots of sunlight. He prepared the soil, removed the rocks, and planted the choicest vines. He built a guard tower in the middle to more easily spot thieves and foraging animals. He hewed a winepress right in the vineyard so the grapes could be squeezed at their peak of freshness. This sounds like a lot of parents I talk to who have sought to create an environment conducive to the spiritual, emotional, psychological, and physical health of their family. Then the keeper expected a crop of good grapes but got only worthless ones. Again, this sounds like healthy families in which people still make unhealthy choices (God seems to give people that option better than we do).

In verse 4, God asked two questions I hear frequently from parents when their children have made choices that are unhealthy and destructive. First, "What more could have been done to My vineyard that I have not done in it?" Second, "Why then, when I expected it to bring forth good grapes, did it bring forth wild grapes?"

Notice what God does *not* do. He does not blame Himself or anyone else. He does not say, "My children have turned out bad, so I must not have been a good enough God." In fact, He does not even answer His two questions at all. What He does is let the vineyard go to ruin.

> And now, please let Me tell you what I will do to My
>   vineyard:
> I will take away its hedge, and it shall be burned;
> and break down its wall, and it shall be trampled
>   down.
> I will lay it waste;
> it shall not be pruned or dug,
> but there shall come up briers and thorns.
> I will also command the clouds
> that they rain no rain on it. (Isa. 5:5–6)

The rest of Isaiah 5, 6, and 7:1–13 contains bad news and pain for the people of God, all because God let go.

Suddenly we come to 7:14 and the reason God let go. Isaiah 7:14 relates to Isaiah 5:1–7:13 as Romans 3:24ff. relates to Romans 1:18–32. Isaiah 7:14 says, "Therefore the Lord Himself will give you a sign: Behold, the virgin shall conceive and bear a Son, and shall call His name Immanuel." Good news! But sometimes the good news does not seem so good when you have been hidden, protected, and rescued from the bad. The sooner a person realizes how inadequate his own resources are, the better. So God lets people go, "gives them up" to their own courses, in order for them to discover how bad the bad news really is.

Deciding a Course of Action

I would like to summarize this chapter by listing a number of principles. These principles will be beneficial to remember when deciding a course to take that will be the most helpful to someone who does not realize his need for help.

1. Family members and others who care need to get out of the "justice business." Many who wish to help spend much of their relationship with a chemically dependent person either making sure that the person gets what he deserves or preventing him from getting what he deserves. Justice is God's business. Romans 12:17–19 says so. Galatians 6:7 says, "Do not be deceived, God is not mocked; for whatever a man sows, that he will also reap." God has His system already in place to see that people receive appropriate consequences for their behavior. Many well-meaning Christians short-circuit God's system when they try to fix others. Most often, our most helpful response is to get out of the way and quit fouling up God's system by rescuing the dependent person, pretending we are not affected, or making excuses to others for his behavior. The best way to convince a person that his life is not working is to let the natural consequences of his behavior teach him.

The ways in which George and Carrie handled the chemically dependent person whose behavior affected them is a good example of fouling up God's system. Carrie's brother Bill had come to live with them. His life was out of control. He was out of money. Former friends were trying to harm him, and he was heavily involved with chemical use. George and Carrie had awareness of the situation and knew what was necessary to make Bill's stay successful. He had stayed with them in the past, and from those visits they had gained a lot of experience with what did *not* work.

Consequently, before this visit, a contract had been drawn up and signed by all three. It contained the terms of the visit. Bill was to carry his load of family chores. He agreed to go to church with the family. He also promised to attend a self-help group for his chemical problem. And of utmost importance, Bill committed to abstain from chemical use during the duration of his stay with Carrie and George.

In less than two months, Bill was failing to keep all of the commitments he had made in order to live with his sister's family. Both George and Carrie responded in an unhealthy manner. George spent all of his energy making excuses for Bill, compensating for his irresponsibility, and letting him off the hook for failing to keep his commitments. Carrie used her time to become a private detective, police officer, prosecuting attorney, and judge. She used her energy to trap him, catch him, weed him out, and convict him. She thought of consequence after consequence, attempting to give him "what he deserved."

George's efforts guaranteed that Bill never had to accept responsibility or face the consequences of his actions. George simply made it possible for Bill to avoid all the changes that he hoped Bill would make. Carrie's actions only angered, hurt, or confused Bill more than he already was. His response was to raise his defenses and pull farther away from his sister. Thus, George and Carrie helped perpetuate the very situation they wished would change.

The most helpful thing George and Carrie could have done would have been for them to hold Bill to their original agreement. This would have had the effect on Bill of making his problem *his* problem. The only hope for genuine change to begin in a person is for him to accept responsibility for his own life and behavior. Such an approach would have allowed George and Carrie to maintain their integrity while enabling them to affirm something on the outside with which they agreed on the inside.

2. Our main responsibility to our dependent loved one is to be healthy ourselves, drawing our life, value, and meaning from Christ as a gift and not as a result of our loved one's performance. This principle is brilliantly illustrated in the exchange between Jesus and Peter in John 21:18–22. Jesus has just let Peter in on some of the details of how Peter would die. Peter, shaken by the description of the path he will take to follow Jesus, points to John and says to Jesus, "But Lord, what about this man?" Jesus replies, "If I will that he remain till I come, what is that to you? You follow Me." I have seen so many codependent people lose their intimacy with Jesus and integrity with others as a result of their preoccupation with the spirituality of their dependent loved one. In the words of Jesus, this other person's spiritual journey is Jesus' issue, not yours. Your spiritual journey is your issue; you follow Him. This is not selfish—it is necessary.

3. Closely associated to this is our responsibility to be an honest, credible person in our relationship with someone who is dependent. This includes meaning what we say and not supporting with our behavior what we do not support in our heart. When the person finally does realize his need for help, he will be looking for a person he can trust to be honest with him. He will need to hear from a person who can confront unacceptable behavior without shaming people on the basis of their behavior.

4. Accepting people "right where they are" does not mean overlooking or excusing where they are. I would like to submit to you that Jesus always accepted people right where they

were. He accepted the blind and lame and made them whole. He accepted the hungry as being hungry and fed them. When He met Pharisees, He accepted them as pompous and self-righteous, right where they were. He responded to them the way you respond to pompous, self-righteous Pharisees. He confronted their self-righteousness and called them hypocrites. He pronounced woes on them and warned others against them. He did not overlook them or excuse them, and He was not bullied by them.

Accepting chemically dependent people right where they are means accepting them as chemically dependent, not over-looking their dependency or excusing their behavior. It means accepting that addiction is there and acting like it. If the persons do not know they have a problem, you accept that and respond in the ways described in this chapter. Hold them accountable for their actions. Don't rescue them from the consequences of their behavior. Don't make excuses. Mean what you say. And find support from individuals or groups who understand the dynamics of addiction and codependency. Your health is your responsibility. On the other hand, if they realize their need, chapter 9 will be more helpful.

5. Real love, agape love—love with no strings attached— is the most beneficial way to approach the chemically dependent person. Agape love does not mean overlooking what is really there. It means loving a person enough to refrain from trying to be his god. This includes ceasing to try to control his behavior as well as to protect him from its consequences. Agape love does not say those things that will keep a person liking you; it does not seek to keep the peace at the expense of the truth. It means saying what is true and trusting God for the results. It means doing what is true simply because it is true, even if you do not believe that the person will respond the way you would like him to. Agape love results from having

one source and one alone, God Himself, instead of your loved one's behavior, your own ability to fix his problem, or people's opinions as they look on.

6. In Mark 7:15–23 Jesus said that what comes out of a man indicates where his heart is. A person's actions will indicate what his intentions are. Actions speak louder than words. Actions are a more accurate indicator of what is in the heart of a chemically dependent person than his words. He will say what he has to in order to keep his chemical use and lifestyle. Therefore, if a chemically dependent person says that he realizes he has a problem but does not seek help, he does not really accept that he has a problem. Neither does he understand the magnitude of his need and his powerlessness to overcome it alone.

But when he finally does realize this, his recovery will really begin. Likewise, when the codependent realizes that her job is not to fix the addict but to get help for herself, her recovery process will also finally begin.

8

Health Can't Be Legislated

The material in this chapter is theological in nature, and it is no easy, quick task to discover a practical application of it. However, I am convinced that an understanding of the following material will be helpful and practical in seeking to help those who are chemically dependent. Reading this chapter will equip you with an understanding to carry through the remaining chapters of the book.

A Firsthand Lesson in Grace

My life was near total disaster when I finally came into a right relationship with God. I was facing the prospect of academic probation at the third (easiest) college I had attended in a period of less than two years. My relationship with my parents was strained because they did not approve of my lifestyle and had threatened to stop supporting it as well as my education. I was arguing and fighting with my roommates, I had lost my job (the third one in less than nine months), and I had resorted to stealing to support myself financially.

After a series of crises, I realized the futility of the way I was living. At that time I also realized that if God was going to look favorably upon me, it would have to be because of something other than myself, for there was nothing in my life that I could point to for the purpose of winning points with God. It would have to be a free gift given to me in spite of my performance. I found life on the basis of Christ's performance.

I think that this acute awareness of the grace that God has shown and continues to show me is the main reason I have been a cheerleader for grace since entering the ministry. I come in contact with individuals and families who are struggling with a variety of problems. Quite frequently I encounter non-Christians who fear that the presence of their problems prevents God from ever having a positive stance toward them. This fear is unfortunate and a total misunderstanding of God. But what I think is more unfortunate is the number of Christians I encounter with problems that they fear negate God's positive stance toward them, as if His positive stance toward them originated from their lack of problems in the first place. This represents as much of a misconception about God as that held by non-Christians.

During my times with these people, my main goal has been to provide an environment and relationship that is grace-full. This experience has been filled with excitement as well as frustration.

The frustration comes because, in spite of the fact that their lives are failing and their relationships have disintegrated, many people simply try harder to overcome their problems through self-support or through formulas, rather than with the support and strength available through grace-full relationships with God and His people. It is interesting, but sad, that oftentimes the ones most resistant to grace are Christians. The excitement comes as people whose problems have broken them, and who are convinced of their powerlessness to generate their own worth, have come to realize the love God has for them, even though they considered themselves utter failures.

When to Preach What

From March 1983 until April 1984, the pastor of our church preached through the book of Galatians. In studying and interacting with that book, and in watching how the apostle Paul dealt with legalism (of all things), I learned one of the most important, practical lessons regarding the ministry. The lesson has had the effect of saving me a lot of time and energy in deciding what message different people need to hear.

Paul understood something about the nature and purpose of the Law that, until this study, I had not. He understood that preaching grace to people who are still under the Law is futile. The fact that they are still under the Law means that the Law is not finished with them yet. Therefore, he preached Law so that the Law could do the work it was given to do. Paul said in Galatians 5:3, "And I testify again to every man who becomes circumcised" (*the attempt to gain God's approval by performing an outward, lawful act*), "that he is a debtor to keep the whole law" (italics mine).

But Paul also understood that preaching the Law to people who are under grace is inappropriate. Thus, he wrote in Galatians 5:1, "Stand fast therefore in the liberty by which Christ has made us free, and do not be entangled again with a yoke of bondage." This lesson is extremely relevant to this discussion because it is in understanding the Law and its function that we can gain great wisdom in knowing how to help and how not to help people who know and do not know they need help.

Law and the Chemically Dependent

You may think it a contradiction to place a chapter having to do with God's law, a subject which is very heavy and theological in nature, in the middle of a book concerned with helping chemically dependent people. It is necessary, however, for two reasons.

First, as we leave chapter 7 and press on to chapter 9, there is a great contrast between the two dispositions of the person we are talking about. The person in chapter 7 does not know he or she has a problem, is convinced that everyone and every-thing else is the problem, and does not see the need for help. The person in chapter 9 has come to realize that his life is not working, that his relationships have failed, that he is powerless to rectify the situation with self-effort, and that he is in need of help. Likewise, there is a great contrast between the approaches used to help that person, depending upon whether chapter 7 or chapter 9 is the better description of him. Those approaches can be characterized by the terms *law-full* and *grace-full*.

Second, from my observations of churches and families that continue to use a law-full approach with repentant people, I conclude that there is great misunderstanding concerning the nature and purpose of the Law, if not theologically, then at least practically. This can have devastating results. The remainder of this chapter is an attempt on my part to provide a basic, accurate understanding of the nature and purpose of the Law, for the purpose of helping those who love chemically depen-dent people to pursue the most helpful, scripturally accurate course when trying to help.

Reasons for the Law

Scripture indicates three purposes for which the Law was given and one purpose for which it was not. The three purposes have to do with God's goal of bringing people into a loving relationship with Himself. The accomplishment of the third goal is the end and fulfillment of the first two. The greatest misunderstanding concerning the Law comes in the area of a perceived purpose that the Law was *not* given to accomplish. The misconception is that the Law is God's provision for people to live victoriously within the relationship with God, assuming that the first three purposes have been accomplished.

First, it is the purpose of the Law to convict people of their shortcomings. The Law was given as a mirror that reflects back to a person the picture that his life is full of sin. Romans 3:20 says, "By the law is the knowledge of sin." In Romans 7:7, Paul said, "I would not have known sin except through the law," and "that sin through the commandment might become exceedingly sinful" (v. 13). When a person has realized through the Law that he is a sinner who has fallen short, it is good.

The second purpose of the Law is to convince people that they cannot come to God by following the Law. The Law is too tough and they are inadequate. Romans 11:32 indicates that the Law was given intentionally to demonstrate our inadequacy: "For God has committed them all to disobedience." How did He do that? He did it through the Law. God created a system that was extremely hard (impossible) to follow, so that when man attempted to follow the system he would always come out a failure. Man would never be able to approach God on the basis of his own performance. Galatians 3:22 reiterates this: "But the Scripture has confined all under sin." The words *committed* and *confined* in both texts convey the sense of being locked in prison. The Law was given, then, not so people could get to God by following it (Rom. 3:20, "By the deeds of the law no flesh will be justified in His sight"), but to show them that they cannot.

The third purpose of the Law is the final one dealing with God's efforts to bring people into a loving relationship with Himself. "God has committed them all to disobedience, that He might have mercy on all" (Rom. 11:32). God has provided a way of coming to a right relationship with Him. The way is one of receiving mercy through faith, not earning mercy by works of the Law. Let me also finish Galatians 3:22–25, my comments in parentheses:

> But the Scripture has confined all under sin, that (*in order that*) the promise by faith (*not by works*) in Jesus Christ might be given to those who believe (*not to those who perform a lot of righteous activity*). But before faith came (*Has it come to you or are you still trying to earn God's approval by what you do?*), we were kept under guard (*restrained*) by the law, kept (*imprisoned*) for the faith which would afterward be revealed. Therefore the law was our tutor to bring us to Christ, that we might be justified by faith. (*And it was revealed.*) But after faith has come, we are no longer under a tutor.

In Matthew 5:17, Jesus reiterated that faith in Him is the goal of the Law: "Do not think that I came to destroy the Law or the Prophets. I did not come to destroy but to fulfill." Faith in Christ is the fulfillment of the Law. Paul supported this in Romans 10:4: "For Christ is the end of the law for righteousness to everyone who believes."

To summarize, then, the three purposes of the Law are aimed at bringing man into a relationship with God. The Law is:

1. to be a measuring rod to demonstrate to man his sin and shortcomings;
2. to represent such an impossible standard to attain that man realizes his inability to do so;
3. to drive man to grace through faith, the only adequate means by which to acquire a positive relationship with God.

That is the reason for such a law-full approach to the person described in chapter 7. The primary need of that person is to come to a place where he realizes that his life is falling short theologically (sin) and practically (broken relationships), that he is incapable through self-effort to hit God's mark and repair all of the damage caused by his unhealthy lifestyle, that he needs help, and that help is available. Consequently, for him to experience the full force of the Law is necessary so that it will be able to do all of its work in his life.

Broken by the Law

Time after time, people come in my office and tell me about how hard it is for them to do all of the things they know they are supposed to be doing. They are simply exhausted from laboring under the Law. They may or may not be Christians, and it may or may not have anything to do specifically with chemical dependency.

I remember one young woman who came to a counseling session, plopped down in the chair, and with her head hung low declared, "I'm tired of being a Christian and I don't know if I can do it anymore!" I think that what she wanted from me was a pep talk. Most people, initially, want some pointers on how to overcome the Law. She wanted me to pump her up with "shoulds" and "try harders" and prop her up with some nice, neat spiritual-sounding formula that would help her live up to God's standard, which always seemed to be indicting her.

I listened as she told me her story. Before she had become a Christian, she had tried to generate self-worth by following the standards of her peer group specifically, and of the world in general. She was following a set of guidelines (evil and fleshly) to try and find value and meaning, using dope, sleeping around, manipulating people for her own gain. This resulted in emptiness for her and pain and problems in her relationships with others, not in the meaningful life for which she had hoped. Through a community-based youth ministry she encountered God's Law, which indicted her, convinced her of her inadequacy to change her situation through her own efforts, and drove her to God's love, a relationship with Christ, and a fresh start. The Law of God had accomplished in her what it was given to do. She began anew under grace. Had she not experienced the full force of the Law, she might not have realized her condition and come to God.

The second part of her story, however, dramatically emphasizes a great misunderstanding people frequently have about the Law. This misunderstanding concerns the correct relationship between the Law and an "under grace" individual. I suspect it explains why many people sense a lack of abundance and joy in their walk with God. I am convinced it explains why many of the efforts of well-meaning people to help the chemically dependent are not effective, and are even a source of further pain and alienation.

As I mentioned, this woman had begun our session by telling me how tired she was from trying to be the kind of Christian she had thought she should be. My response to her tiredness (the same response she would have received had she not been a Christian) shocked her. I exclaimed, "Good! It's good that you're tired." I explained to her that during her pre-Christian days she had tried to find life by pursuing what was an inadequate course: negative self-effort. Since life, value, and meaning are not to be found in that course, she had come up empty and tired. Then she realized that her life was out of line with God's standard and that if she were to have value and meaning in life, they would be found in a relationship with God. An equally important realization was that it would have to be on the basis of something other than her own ability to live up to the standard. She had received Christ by faith.

Where Is That Sense of Blessing?

At this point in our conversation, I asked her to try to remember how she felt when she first came to know Jesus. She responded with words such as *free*, *relieved*, *joy*, and *light*. I then asked her to compare how she had felt then to how she felt now. She said there was no comparison and she was sad to have somehow lost her sense of joy in the Christian life. I explained to her that after experiencing grace she had simply returned to an old course of action to try to generate life, value, and meaning. She reacted strongly against this statement and began to tell me of the wonderful Christian behavior she had acquired since becoming a Christian. "Then why are you so tired, to the point of wanting to give up?" I asked. She did not know.

At this point, I was able to help her understand that the problem with her old negative self-effort was not the "negative" part but the "self-effort" part. It is not possible to generate worth with self-effort, negative or positive. Galatians 3:21 reads, "If there had been a law given which could have given life, truly righteousness would have been by the law." So even though she had changed many of her unlawful ways into lawful ways, she was attempting to accomplish something with self-effort that is impossible, to find life and generate value and meaning as a human being.

The reason she was feeling so tired is that she had misunderstood the purpose of the Law, had gone back to living under it, and was again experiencing what the Law was given to cause people to experience: guilt and exhaustion. She had tried to find intimacy with God by performing the works of the Law, something the Law was never intended to give, and was constantly living under the Law's indictment.

Misapplying the Law

The phrase "grace-full" is one I have used several times already, and it is going to appear quite frequently in the rest of the book. When I say it, I mean "full of grace," characterized by grace, communicating grace. I am explaining this now, because ultimately, the Law is intimately related to the grace of God. I am baffled about how Christians can be acutely aware that following the Law cannot make them righteous in the first place, but have no awareness that victory in their lives and God's stance toward them after they have become a Christian does not, likewise, depend upon their performance of the Law.

Many Christians are trying to find the abundant life under the uncompromising Law that demands perfection and in the difficult, impossible Law that cannot give it, and even prevents it. "For as many as are of the works of the law are under the curse; for it is written, 'Cursed is everyone who does not continue in all things which are written in the book of the law, to do them'" (Gal. 3:10). "For the law made nothing perfect" (Heb. 7:19). Not only are they trying to please God by performing the Law, but they are putting other people back under the Law as well. This can be a frustrating way to live.

Putting God to the Test

In Acts 15:5–11, a debate occurs about whether to put Gentile Christians under the Law in order for them to be considered genuine believers. Peter's response in verses 9 and 10 indicates what he thought about living under the Law:

And (He) made no distinction between us and them, purifying their hearts by faith (*not through the observance of the law*). Now therefore, why do you test God by putting a yoke (*the Law*) on the neck of the disciples which neither our fathers nor we were able to bear? (italics mine)

Peter's assessment of putting people back under the Law who come to grace (the Gentile Christians, in this case) was that it is "putting God to the test." Why? Because it is acting as if God has not really done enough through Christ to establish our right relationship with Him, as if there is something we must do in addition. For a person to assess that his life is victorious based upon how well he has followed the Law indicates that his source of satisfaction is himself, derived from his own successful self-effort. This is idolatrous; it leads to self-righteousness, and it is not what God intended.

Joined by Faith to Christ through Grace

The purpose of the Law is not to restrain evil people. The Law was given to convict evil people. The purpose of the Law is not to motivate or control people who are righteous in Christ. The Law was given to drive man to grace and leave him there. The victorious life is not to be found in, under, or through the Law. It is to be discovered and lived under grace, in grace-full environments and through grace-full relationships with Jesus Christ and others.

Therefore, if the Law has really accomplished its purpose, it will have worked itself out of a job. And if you are a Christian, that is exactly what the Law has done. Galatians 2:19 says, "For I through the law died to the law that I might live to God." In 3:24–25, Paul said, "Therefore the law was our tutor to bring us to Christ, that we might be justified by faith.

But after faith has come, we are no longer under a tutor (*the Law*)" (italics mine).

Romans 7:4–6 not only affirms this but indicts the methods many parents, teachers, and pastors use to cause people to act in positive ways.

> Therefore, my brethren, you also have become dead to the law through the body of Christ, that you may be married to another, even to Him who was raised from the dead, that we should bear fruit to God. For when we were in the flesh, the passions of sins which were aroused by the law were at work in our members to bear fruit to death. But now we have been delivered from the law, having died to what we were held by, so that we should serve in the newness of the Spirit and not in the oldness of the letter (*of the Law*). (italics mine)

In this passage Paul indicated two things that need to happen in order for a person to produce fruit for God. First, one must be made to die to the Law. Second, one must be joined to Christ. By grace through faith, we die to the Law and are joined to Christ so that we can produce fruit for God. Fruit is not produced as the result of adherence to some external code of ethics, which we can never completely follow anyway, but in and through the Spirit who lives within us.

Trying to Legislate Health

Unfortunately, one of the primary ways I see parents and others in the Christian community trying to motivate the right behavior in people is to put them back under that Law from which Christ died to free them. This, also, is probably the most frequent and unhelpful way that Christians try to support chemically dependent people who have come to realize their need for help.

In Galatians 3:1–3, Paul confronted the Galatians for trying to find fullness and success in life by following the Law. He called them fools and insinuated that they had been bewitched for holding such a notion.

> O foolish Galatians! Who has bewitched you that you should not obey the truth, before whose eyes Jesus Christ was clearly portrayed among you as crucified? This only I want to learn from you: Did you receive the Spirit by the works of the law, or by the hearing of faith (*a rhetorical question with the answer: hearing with faith*)? Are you so foolish? Having begun in the Spirit, are you now being made perfect by the flesh? (italics mine)

The reason this is such a confrontation is that in the third verse the Galatians were, indeed, trying to be perfected by the flesh (or through their own self-effort, which corresponds directly to "works of the law"). In the second verse, Paul was reminding them that they should live on the same basis upon which they had entered a relationship with God in the first place: faith.

Internal vs. External Constraint

You may be asking at this point, "If you take the Law off people, what is going to control their behavior? What will get them to do good things?" The answer, if the person has really come to Christ, is faith. Galatians 2:20 says, "I have been crucified with Christ; it is no longer I who live, but Christ lives in me; and the life which I now live in the flesh I live by faith in the Son of God." Paul rejoiced over the Christians at Colossae who were demonstrating good discipline and stability in their faith (see Col. 2:5), and he urged them to continue walking in the same way as they received Christ in the first place, which was by faith (see v. 6).

In 2 Corinthians 5:14, Paul said, "For the love of Christ constrains us." This does not mean that we are so grateful that Christ loves us that we do lots of good things to pay Him back. It means that we have experienced Christ's love, we are full, and we understand who we are and what we have because of having experienced that love. Out of the fullness of being loved by Jesus, we do what we do. Once again, it boils down to faith in Christ.

Faith in Christ and dependence upon Him as the sole source of life, value, and meaning, take the place of trying to gain, earn, acquire, or protect life and worth from any other source. Obviously, then, faith in sex, drugs, power, people's opinions, money, property, status, and so forth, is not what gives meaning.

Not so obvious to some, however, is the fact that neither is it faith in religion, or positive self-effort (the fact that now we are trying to follow a better set of rules then we used to) that makes us OK. Putting faith in anything other than Christ as our source of all life amounts to idolatry. It is sad to see how frequently people are discipled in performance of certain ways to act, but not in having faith in Christ alone as their source of life. Putting "God" labels on self-effort just makes self-effort harder to confront. It's not Jesus first. It's Jesus only. It's not "things go better with Christ." It's "things only go with Christ."

Don't Be Squeezed!

The problem is that trusting God alone as our only source is difficult. To trust God this way means going against the value of society that says people find life in and through their own efforts (how much we own, how we dress, how we look, how much money we have, who likes us, and who we know makes us valuable people). This kind of trust may even mean going against the grain of churches and other Christians who urge us to find value and meaning in our own positive self-effort (how disciplined we are, how much we give, how much we read our Bible, how many times we attend church, and what denomination we belong to makes us valuable people).

We desperately need grace-full relationships and a grace-full environment that affirms who we are and what we have based upon Christ's performance and not on ours (and sometimes in spite of ours). When a Christian family comes to me for help with family dysfunction, I have them understand that they are so valuable in Christ that they can even tell me what a mess their family is. Mistakes and problems do not have the power to devaluate people under grace. As they come to believe that fact, they are set free to talk about the problems that they once felt changed God's stance toward them. Through this support, people can learn to live in a way that is consistent with who they already are and what they already have.

Living Consistently with Christ's Victory

The Greek language is rich and communicates messages full of meaning that sometimes get lost in translation to English. Let's examine Hebrews 10:10 and 14 (italics mine):

> By that will we have been sanctified (*In the Greek language, "have been sanctified" is a perfect passive participle. It means that sanctification is something done to us, not something we do through any action of our own, that in Christ the process of our sanctification has been completed and we are still experiencing the results of that on an ongoing basis.*

And "sanctified" is not only the action done to us but also a description of us.) through the offering of the body of Jesus Christ once for all. For by one offering He has perfected ("Has perfected" is a process that has been completed and we are, once again, still experiencing the consequences of that action by Christ.) forever those who are being sanctified. ("Who are being sanctified" indicates that at every point in the present we are sanctified. "Sanctified" describes the action and also the "who," which in this case is "we.")

Grace-full relationships affirm who people are on the basis of what God has already done, not what they do based upon external expectations. They encourage people to live in a manner that is consistent with who they are and what they already have because of what God has done through Christ. "Nevertheless, to the degree that we have already attained, let us walk by the same rule" (Phil. 3:16). The Greek indicates that we are to live, not to attain the standard, but in a way that is consistent with a standard already attained.

Grace-full relationships provide a safe place for people to take the risks necessary for growth without the fear of being indicted by failures. They represent a firsthand, flesh-and-blood experience of what it means to be accepted by God on the basis of something other than personal performance, an experience that is nonexistent in the world and all too rare in many families and churches.

9

Helping Those Who Know They Need It

At the beginning of chapter 7, I talked about the five ingredients that are necessary for a chemically dependent person to begin and sustain a recovery. Later in this chapter I will talk about these ingredients in a more specific fashion. Before that, however, I wish to discuss two general principles that will help people be more effective helpers.

In chapter 3, I listed four areas of dysfunction in the lives of the chemically dependent. *Spiritually*, they have turned to chemicals or their own selves as a god. *Emotionally*, they have denied and frozen their pain. *Psychologically*, an elaborate defense system has been developed to hide their shame. And *physically*, their health may be in jeopardy. Recall, also, that I mentioned that these four areas usually become affected in the order in which I listed them. In addition, needs and dysfunction in each area tend to mask needs in the areas preceding it.

Answer Questions People Are Asking

Keeping these things in mind, let us consider a passage of Scripture found in Matthew. Matthew 9:2–8 tells of a paralytic who was brought to Jesus for healing. Jesus' response was not one that the crowd expected. "Son, be of good cheer; your sins are forgiven" (v. 2). Jesus' forgiveness of the paralytic caused a considerable stir among the religious types who accused Jesus of blasphemy. In defense of His actions, Jesus made a series of statements that are relevant to this discussion. In verses 5–6 we read:

> "For which is easier, to say, 'Your sins are forgiven you,' or to say, 'Arise and walk'? But that you may know that the Son of Man has power on earth to forgive sins"—then He said to the paralytic, "Arise, take up your bed, and go to your house."

Jesus made His point with a hypothetical question. Obviously, telling someone that his sins are forgiven is easier than telling a crippled person to rise and walk. No one would be able to tell if the sins actually had been forgiven, should you lack that ability. However, if nothing happened when you told the person he was healed, everyone would know you were a fake. To demonstrate His authority in the spiritual realm, so that people would know He did have the answer to spiritual needs, He performed an act in the physical realm.

Very often, we as Christians think that the spiritual need is the only important, official need. In our zeal to meet that need, we miss many opportunities for ministry in the other areas I have mentioned. In addition, very often our lack of success in the area of meeting spiritual needs is due to the fact that we are perceived as being irrelevant because of our lack of involvement in the other areas.

Not only this, but often the person needing help is so preoccupied with his pain in another area that any need or pain in a preceding area is not felt. Therefore, to try to meet needs that a person does not realize he has is not a wise use of time or energy. Meeting a person's felt need in any given area is valid ministry, because it demonstrates care and relevance (as opposed to spiritual superiority) and very possibly will gain the helper permission to continue to minister in other areas of need at a later date.

Address the Primary Problem

The second general principle can be illustrated with a story. One day while I was at my home, I received a telephone call from California. The caller was a woman unknown to me. She had never heard me speak in person, and I do not know how she got my telephone number. She began to tell me of her experiences with her husband who was an alcoholic. She told me that they were going to Christian marriage counseling, where they discussed with their counselor the problems they were having in their marriage: communication, sexual, parenting, and financial.

They seemed to make great progress, and she was amazed at how open and willing to change her husband seemed in counseling. She was bewildered and discouraged, because for about two weeks after each session (evidently they were going semi-monthly), everything would be fine. But then things always seemed to return to how they were before, and she could not understand why. I asked her if anything was ever said about her husband's drinking. Her answer was that neither she nor the counselor believed it was necessary in light of his two good weeks following each session. They had felt that perhaps the drinking was not that big of an issue, and that the husband simply needed to try harder to follow the formulas prescribed in counseling.

To understand the dilemma I have just described, try to picture chemical dependency as a balance scale. On one side of the scale is the chemical use and on the other are certain behaviors, attitudes, and feelings.

The elements on the two sides of the scale balance each other nicely. In order for a person to recover from chemical dependency, all of the elements must be addressed. If they are not, the stage is set for the problem to return. For instance, if the person simply quits drinking (which all too often is the only goal of most "help"), the behaviors, attitudes, and feelings that nourish the dependency remain.

This causes an imbalance. In order for a person to be able to feel comfortable again, he may begin to acquire new behaviors, attitudes, and feelings that are more compatible with a chemical-free lifestyle. Or he could return to alcohol or his other drug of choice, which would also bring "comfort." This can be compared to a teenager who goes to summer camp and rededicates his life to God. When he returns home, however, he forms no new relationships, learns no new skills for living, and acquires no new attitudes. When he returns to his former ways, many people doubt the sincerity of his rededication. His problem was not that he was insincere; it was that he did not learn how to live.

The aforementioned telephone call demonstrates the other side of the same coin. The couple's situation is a good illustration of another imbalance that does not lead to health. This imbalance occurs when the chemical use continues at the same time help is being sought.

In the case of the husband who was making great strides in overcoming his marital difficulties (drinking the whole time), the acquisition of new behaviors, attitudes, and feelings that were more conducive to a nonusing lifestyle created discomfort. One way to help restore comfort would have been for the husband to abstain from chemical use. However, since the use of chemicals was never addressed, old behaviors, attitudes, and feelings won out over his trying-hard approach to health.

The Process of Recovery

Having said these things, let me proceed to delineate the five specific steps needed to be taken for the chemically dependent person to have a quality recovery. I mentioned them at the beginning of chapter 7. They are:

1. The dependent person must realize he needs help.
2. He needs to find a way to get from the spiritual and emotional pit to normal without having to use chemicals to do it.
3. He must undergo emotional healing.
4. The delusion in which he had lived must be shattered.
5. He needs to learn or relearn healthy living skills in order to live a healthy, productive life.

Of course, talking about ways to help this happen in the life of a person who does not know he needs it to happen is pointless. Therefore, as we approach the rest of this chapter, let us assume that we are talking about a person who knows he needs help. When a person realizes that he needs help, the battle is half over!

The Purpose of Confession
Is to Receive Forgiveness

Once a person knows he has a problem and realizes his need for help, to continue to treat him as someone who still thinks that his unhealthy way of life is fine is harmful and unscriptural.

You will notice in the end of the story of the prodigal son that when the son returned home, he received a party. He did not get a sermon or hear the highlights of his misadventures. Once he had come to his senses, he was forgiven and restored, and there was a celebration.

Another passage of Scripture that supports this idea is 2 Corinthians 2:6–8. The verses refer to the man referred to by Paul in 1 Corinthians 5:1–7. Paul told the church to cast a man from their midst so that the pain inflicted by the rejection might help him to wake up and see his impropriety. But 2 Corinthians 2:6–8 seems to indicate that the man repented. Notice Paul's advice regarding that man.

> This punishment which was inflicted by the majority is sufficient for such a man, so that, on the contrary, you ought rather to forgive and comfort him, lest perhaps such a one be swallowed up with too much sorrow. Therefore I urge you to reaffirm your love for him.

Jesus' response to the woman taken in adultery, "Neither do I condemn you; go and sin no more" (John 8:11), affirms this. The point is that it is wrong, even though it might feel good to you, to continue to cause sorrow with reminders, indictments, or sermons to persons who have realized they have needs and are seeking help. They have taken the first of the five steps.

Recovering "Grace-fully"

Steps two through five, then, are the next part of the recovery process. That the dependent persons are seeking help in the first place means they have looked at themselves in a new light, an honest light. The realization that everyone and everything else is not the cause of their misery has caused them to seek a course to change their lives. But there is more work to do. They need to continue to understand the ways in which they have become dishonest, manipulative, defensive, blaming, and rigid (with respect to self and others).

They must face, with brutal honesty, the pain and humiliation they have caused those they love the most. They must continue to see the ways they have justified (to self and others) destructive actions and attitudes, trying to convince everyone that what is wrong is right. However, there is a difference between the self-realization of inappropriateness in a person who is trying to get healthy and the indictments and constant badgering and mistrust people continue to give them even after they have repented. Even healthy self-assessment for a person who has hidden and compromised is a very threatening prospect.

Emotionally, pain has been denied and frozen with the use of chemicals and with dishonesty in relationships. Anger, fear, resentment, guilt, sadness, and shame need to be shared, not stored. Too often I find people in my office who equate not showing feelings with not having them. They think that if they do not act angry, others (God, for instance) will not know they are angry. Many people have grown up in such painful family situations that they have been conditioned not to acknowledge or show their feelings. They are emotionally stunted. Sometimes they parade the ability not to feel and the ability not to show their feelings as measures of their spirituality.

Clinically, I have found that pretending not to feel certain things is equally as inappropriate as letting feelings come out in harmful ways. It just looks better. But like the self-assessment mentioned before, it is an incredibly threatening prospect to begin to share feelings that have previously been avoided at all costs. However, both are extremely necessary, beneficial aspects of starting anew.

Grace to Get Healthy

Where do people get the strength to be able to take these steps, threatening as they are? While I spent a significant amount of time near the end of chapter 7 discussing this in general, the answer is relationships, grace-full relationships with Christ and His followers. Through a relationship with Jesus Christ, a person can find the gift of life, value, and meaning. Only life and worth received for free on the basis of Christ's performance can erase the messages of shame so deeply engrained by lack of personal performance in life and relationships. Only from a place of Christ-earned value can individuals take the kind of personal inventory that will lay bare the psychological dishonesty that has kept them and others fooled for so long. Such an inventory from any other than a grace-full place would prove too big a self-indictment and further cement the shame. From spirituality based upon Christ (and not on the ability to pretend not to feel things), frozen and hidden emotions can be shared and support sought for the emotional pain chemical use and denial once numbed.

Oughtful Information vs. Grace-full Interaction

As I said in chapter 8, such unconditional love, based on the one giving it and not on the performance of the one receiving it, is nonexistent in society and rare in many churches and Christian families. The fact that relationships that provide unconditional love and acceptance are hard to find simply emphasizes the profound necessity for Christian families and churches to be grace-full.

Information does not indict people, neither does it cement shame. People are indicted and shamed by their own lack of perfection as their performance is compared to God's Law (or the law of society, their family, or themselves, if God is not in the picture). There will *always* be a standard that indicts and shames. This is then cemented by relationships that affirm worth and identity based on positive performance (of which there is never enough) and indict or shame on the basis of negative performance (of which there only has to be one instance).

Consequently, information is not capable of erasing shame and cementing value. Only grace-full relationships are capable of modeling the forgiveness and cementing the value that is available because of the death of Christ, because they affirm people's identity based on Christ's performance. Grace-full relationships have the power to demonstrate in a practical way what it means to be an accepted person. This is not something to be taken lightly. In fact, I believe it is one of the hallmarks of living under grace.

In chapter 7, I used the text in Matthew 18 to talk about how to help people realize they have a problem. Now I would like to use it to demonstrate how to help those who have been broken by the Law and have come over to grace. In Matthew 18:18, Jesus says, "Assuredly, I say to you, whatever you bind on earth will be bound in heaven; and whatever you loose on earth will be loosed in heaven." Many people think this means that the disciples somehow had the power to determine what is confirmed in heaven by what they confirmed here.

Upon closer examination of the text, however, you will find that the Greek perfect tense of the words "bound" and "loosed" indicates that the power the disciples really had was to make things on earth consistent with how they are in heaven.

John 20:23 is a text that clearly supports this. "If you forgive the sins of any, they are forgiven them (*have previously been forgiven, in the Greek*); if you retain the sins of any, they are (*already*) retained" (italics mine). Jesus did not mean that the disciples actually had the power to forgive or retain

169

someone's sins. Only God can do that. His statement simply makes the same point as Matthew 18:18: You have the ability to confirm in your relationships with people what is already true about them in heaven. Let us be certain, therefore, that if God has accepted a person based on Christ's performance, our relationship with him is consistent with and cements that which is already true about him as far as God is concerned.

It would be naïve to think that because a person realizes his need for help from his chemical dependency, he also realizes his need for Jesus Christ. It would be equally naïve to think that in order for a person to recover, he first needs to have a relationship with Christ. Many people realize their need and recover with no knowledge of Christ whatsoever. However, this does not negate their need for Him, and the need for Christians to provide grace-full relationships with recovering people. Within the context of these grace-full relationships with Christ and others, the recovering person can move on to the next phase of rebuilding his life.

Health through Grace-full Discipleship

The final aspect of recovery is the acquisition of healthy living skills in order to live a healthy, productive life. This is just a fancy way to say "discipleship." Unfortunately, in our society adulthood implies that when a person is 17 years, 364 days old, he is not an adult, but when he is 17 years, 365 days old, he is. This concept has nothing to do with sensitivity, maturity, responsibility, wisdom, or being able to anticipate ahead of time the consequences of certain behavior. It is just a matter of living a day longer to be able to vote, enlist, use tobacco, and be held accountable for adult decisions.

As a counselor who tries to help people regain the life-style and living skills destroyed by their chemical problems or other problem behavior, I find it interesting that most people I counsel never had healthy living skills to begin with. They never knew how to ask for help when they needed it or give it when needed by someone else. They never sought help for their pain; indeed, they spent most of their effort hiding it. They never were equipped with a variety of problem-solving mechanisms with which to cope with problems in life. In short, there is no health for them to regain. Most people have to begin to learn, at whatever age I see them, what they should have learned from ages one to eighteen.

In Matthew 12:43–45, Jesus told a parable of an unclean spirit that went out of a man and sought rest unsuccessfully.

> When an unclean spirit goes out of a man, he goes through dry places, seeking rest, and finds none. Then he says, "I will return to my house from which I came." And when he comes, he finds it empty, swept, and put in order. Then he goes and takes with him seven other spirits more wicked then himself, and they enter and dwell there; and the last state of that man is worse than the first.

I am not including this text to assert that chemical dependency is a matter of demon possession. I include it for two reasons. First, the parable may explain why, in the phenomenon of relapse, people who begin to use chemicals again seldom start the process over again (see chapter 2). More often than not, they begin very close to the point at which they hit bottom and continue from there. Second, this story clearly indicates the principle that old behaviors, attitudes, and feelings must be replaced by new ones. It is not a matter of simply bringing a person to the point of being neutral. That is not enough. Discipleship is a vital part of the Christian life and a key to recovery from chemical dependency.

10

Help and Hope
for Those Who Love Them

So Much Opportunity for Ministry

What mistakes we have made in the Christian community!
We have focused our attention on chemical use as the problem in chemically dependent families. We have assumed that
when the use of chemicals has ceased the issue is over, for
the dependent person and for members of the family. At one
time, I received a letter that stands as a blistering confrontation of our shallow approach to chemical dependency. Here
are some excerpts that will lay a foundation for the rest of
the chapter.

Dear Jeff,

I am so confused and so is he [the alcoholic]. I can't stand
him around me. He flutters, and struts, and kiddingly cuts
me down. Then when I get angry, he laughs at me and hugs
or squeezes me and tells me I'm so cute and beautiful and
how much he loves me. He's so puffed up and egotistical.
He's drowning me with superficial affection. I can't tell him,

because I feel like I'll hurt him, even though he's abused me so much.

He thinks he's all better now, and that I'm all better now, and we're a happy family again. Wow, what a lie! The pastor said to both of us yesterday, "You two look so much happier now." All I could do was fake a smile. Inside I was really crying. Two days ago I started hyperventilating while telling my girlfriend about my anger toward [the alcoholic]. I feel more in despair now than I did the first time I broke down in July! I'm supposed to be growing in Christ, but how can I? I love the Lord so much, and I know this takes time, but I am so anxious and frustrated. I have quit moving.

I can't forget this and I don't know how to handle it. I just want to kill [crossed out] destroy him for all the things he's done and said to me. But oh, wait. He's sick, isn't he? That's the big excuse I get. Then I should understand. Well, I can't understand! He still abuses me, in a kindly way. I wish he would go away and leave me alone.

I used to watch my dad try to strangle my mom when he was drunk. He tried to shoot her in the head with a shotgun and drown her head in the toilet. Now I can see why I am the way I am. I knew no other way, until I became a Christian.

Give me a corner all by myself and a big fluffy pillow to hold on to. I know I'll feel so good. I can just picture myself in a carpeted room all by myself in the corner. I pray each day, all day long, and I know God is there. But I hurt so deep. I feel like I need someone to hold my hand and walk me through this. I am so afraid to move on in this life all by myself, and yet I can't let my family down either. My children need me, but they need me healthy too.

My plan in this chapter is to present a practical, in-depth discussion on how to help those family members and friends whose lives have been affected in negative, hurtful ways because they have cared about someone who is chemically dependent. There have been books written on this subject alone, and I am painfully aware of the complexity and magnitude of the problems in a family that has had to learn to live with chemical dependency.

I am equally aware of the fact that families do not get well by reading books. My opinion is that upon discovering that your family has begun to look and sound like the system described in chapters 3 and 4, the healthiest course of action for you is to seek professional help. In this chapter I am not trying to fix families. Instead, my goal is to provide some general principles and some specific guidelines that will be beneficial when it comes time for you to give or receive help.

Things Are Not Always as They Seem

In addition to complexity and magnitude, a factor that complicates things even more is the delusion of the codependent family members. In other words, because the family members are deluded, things may not always be as they appear to the one offering help. Sometimes people live in ways that are destructive and painful to themselves and others for reasons that never surface and are hard to track down and address. I cannot stress enough the need to remember this as we go through this chapter or as you try to help a family who has been in the grips of chemical dependency. In order for you to have more of an appreciation of this concept, I would like to relate two situations, one I was told about by another counselor and the other I discovered in one of my own sessions.

A family had two girls who were in their early teens. One of them wanted nothing to do with males; she acted as if she hated her brothers and father. She expressed no interest in dating and indicated that she might never date. She had a reputation at school for being unfriendly. She dressed very plainly and barely kept herself presentable. Her sister, on the other hand, was promiscuous. She dressed suggestively, wore heavy makeup, hung on any guy who would give her the slightest bit of attention, and had a bad reputation.

The family was concerned for both of them (the second daughter more than the first, however). Why did they act that way? What could cause daughters in the same family to turn out so different?

After some counseling with the daughters and involvement with the family, it was discovered that their father was a very distant, unemotional man who always seemed complacent about his daughters' lives. When they were little he never hugged, bounced, wrestled with, or kissed them. He did not provide a relationship for them in which they could ask questions about life or seek advice. He acted apathetic when they sought direction. He was uninvolved when it came to disciplining them. In fact, their whole upbringing had been the responsibility of the mother.

Consequently, the girls had grown up lacking healthy male affection and intimacy. The first daughter interpreted the lack of affection and attention as rejection, gave up, and transferred her disdain for her father to all males. She learned that no matter how hard she tried, she could never do enough, so why try? The second daughter interpreted the lack of affection and attention as rejection, gave up on her father, and transferred her efforts to experience affection and intimacy to any male she could get to notice her.

But what about the father? Why did he act that way? What could have caused him to be so neglectful of his own daughters' legitimate needs?

Some more counseling and involvement with the family revealed that the father had grown up in a family where his father was overbearing and demanding with his wife and children, especially the daughters. No matter how hard they tried, they could never do enough. He saw how his sisters were constantly discouraged, depressed, hurt, and shamed by his father's uncompromising demands. Then one day he discovered the ultimate horror. His father was having sexual intercourse with his sisters and had convinced them that if they told anyone, the grief would destroy their mother and ruin the marriage. So they kept the secret and became more and more weighted down by the weight of "their" sin.

After seeing the traumatic effects that his father's behavior had on his own sisters, he vowed that if he ever had daughters of his own, he would *never* do to them what his father did to his sisters. Unfortunately, his inappropriate *under*involvement had the same effects on his daughters that his father's inappropriate *over*involvement had on his sisters. More was involved here than the anti-male behavior of one teenager and the promiscuity of another.

Another Slippery Case

In a session not too long ago, I discovered some equally slippery motives and problems in a family. The solution to the problems that were presented initially might have smoothed them over temporarily, but would have actually perpetuated the real problems that had merely been masked by those on the surface.

The son was chemically dependent, had completed treatment, and was using again. He had graduated from high school by the skin of his teeth and planned to attend college in the fall. He had gotten two jobs for the summer, one selling vacuum cleaners and another at a grocery store. Up to the point of our session, he had sold only one vacuum cleaner and was constantly absent from or late for his grocery job. He was out of money for gas and dates. He had nothing saved for his college needs. He was in danger of losing the grocery job. He continued to use chemicals, sleep late in the mornings, lie around the house in the afternoons while family members catered to or stayed away from him, and avoided members of the family in the evening until he could manage to go out to a bar or party.

The reason for this particular session was that the mother and son were fighting like cats and dogs, and the parents could not agree on the best approach to the situation. The mother continued to defend her nagging, screaming, pleading, and guilt trips on the grounds of her concern that the son was not learning to be responsible for himself. She believed that he needed to become responsible immediately (there was, after all, only a little time left until college), and that was why she was always on his back. She was angry at the father because he was always giving the son the benefit of the doubt, fronting him money, extending deadlines, and urging the mother to leave him alone. The mother thought the father was enabling the son to continue to be irresponsible.

The father defended his financial support of the son, his trying to calm the mother, his compromising the deadlines, and his lack of confronting negative behavior on the grounds that people do not become responsible overnight. He thought his son needed encouragement, support, someone to smooth out the rough spots a little, a troubleshooter to help the young man get started in this dog-eat-dog world. He was angry at the mother for being such a pessimist and for being so critical of the lad.

After some time in counseling, the real reasons for the parents' acting the way they were slipped out in the heat of a frustrating moment. The mother had said that she was concerned about her son's college spending-money situation, his lack of ambition and motivation, his constant partying, his relationship with his siblings, and his father's apparent fostering of his irresponsible behavior.

The real reason, however, for her constant nagging and indictments was that she was just plain tired of having him around. Seeing him lie around all day with a hangover disgusted her. Trying to explain to her other children the "good" reasons (there were really only unhealthy ones) why this son was able to do what he was doing without consequences wore her out. Watching the father continually coddle and rescue the son angered her. She was tired of the hassles, tired of the son, tired of the father, and just wanted the son gone so she could have some peace. And now it looked as if he might not even be able to go to college and so would still be at home in the fall.

The father, on the other hand, had his own concealed reasons for "helping" the son. The father had said that he was only buying the son the time he needed to get started. He was simply being more patient with the son than was the mother. He understood responsibility cannot be rushed, that a person needs a steadying hand as he goes through the school of hard knocks.

Behind all of the father's benevolence, however, lay the real motives. He was tired of spending all of his time mediating the relationship between his wife and son. He was tired of being mortified in the middle of executive meetings by calls from the mother about the son, from the son about the mother. He was tired of his wife's complaining about the son's laziness. He was tired of his son's complaining about his wife's nagging. He was tired of his wife's nagging him to start holding the son accountable.

His solution was to overlook as much as possible and give the son enough money to get him out of the house as often as possible. That cut down on the amount of time the mother and son had together. This, in turn, reduced the amount of time the mother observed the delinquent son, which eliminated some of the mother's nagging and the son's defensiveness. Consequently, the father did not have to mediate as much or listen to as much complaining as when the son was around all of the time.

The scariest part about the whole thing is that the hidden reasons were not obvious to either parent without a significant amount of digging, nor were they easy to admit once discovered.

People's Health Is Their Own Responsibility

Recall now the beginning of chapter 4 where I said that there are three essential ingredients that need to be present for a person to be affected by someone else's chemical dependency: caring for the person; being unaware or ill-aware of the problem; living with shame. When parents come in to talk about the turmoil in their family because of the chemical use of a son or daughter, when a wife or husband begins to tell about the traumatic ways their lives are being affected by the chemical use of a spouse, when teenagers share their fear concerning their parent's drinking, very early into the process I begin to head them in the direction of their own health.

Where these three ingredients are present, there are sure to be unhealthy people in much pain. That empty people can affirm other empty people with any motivation other than for the purpose of trying to fill themselves is a ludicrous thought. Very often in a family where there is chemical dependency, unhealthy people are caring for another unhealthy person. Our goal is to have healthy people caring for the unhealthy person. If this goal can be accomplished, the recovering person will have a healthy system to return to.

The reason caring has been a problem has not been because people have cared. The ingredient of caring has become a problem because of the presence of the other two ingredients.

First, those who care have never learned to care in a way that is helpful to the dependent person and not harmful to themselves. They have been uninformed or ill-informed as to the nature of the problem and maybe even oblivious to its presence. Therefore, the problem went on much longer than it needed to, or it was dealt with as if it were something other than what it was.

Many times people need things to be a certain way so badly that they simply see them that way. They keep treating a spouse or child the way they wish they were instead of accepting them the way they really are. This is rejecting. Shame contributes to this phenomenon too, because if the presence of a problem in the family shames the family members, it is easier not to see the problem.

It's OK to Seek Help

If you notice changes in people and problems in your relationships with family members, going to a counselor to get help is not always necessary. Many things can be worked out within a family. However, if after reasonable attempts and a reasonable amount of time things do not get better, seek help. The key lies in setting a limit as to how much time and effort will be invested without improvement, then sticking to the limit. When the limit is reached, seek help from a trained professional.

If you do not know exactly what the problem is, consult a professional trained in assessment and diagnosis. If you know what the problem is, seek a person or program that specializes in helping people with that particular problem. Do not go over your limit. Do not act as if you have been trained as a chemical dependency counselor. Chemically dependent people have a lot at stake to keep their problem, and on your best day they can send you on a merry wild goose chase.

It Helps to Know What the Problem Is

I remember one particular seminar I gave to fifty Baptist pastors. Suddenly, as I was describing the family of a dependent person, a pastor sitting near the front grabbed the sides of his head with both hands, dropped his face to the desk, and moaned, "Ooh!" His reaction was rather violent, and for a split second I actually thought that he had suffered a stroke or something. Finally, he picked his head up, dropped his hands to the desk, and looked me straight in the eyes. Then for a brief moment, I thought he was going to rebuke me in the name of the Lord.

Instead, with a slight tremble in his voice, he said, "We are failing these people so miserably!" He went on to say that I had just described a family he had been counseling for the past five years (for the wrong problems) with no apparent progress. He concluded by saying that he wished he had known twenty-five years ago what he had just learned, as he believed that many people would have been helped and much time saved.

A Bothersome Question

As I said before, family members and others who care have acted as if unhealthy people unconcerned with their own health can help other unhealthy people become healthy. That is why I raise the question about their own health, independent of the health and recovery of their loved one. To do it I might ask a question like this: "What are you going to do to be a healthy person, even if _____ never gets better?"

This statement suggests that family members can and must find health and a sense of peace and well-being somewhere other than from the successes and failures of their dependent loved one. It also opens the door for me to begin to talk about each person's lack of health, their inappropriate motives for caring, and the shame they are experiencing because of their situation (or the shame they had even before the situation ever developed).

The question usually bothers a lot of people too. They do not want to talk about the family as a system and the health of the individual members that comprise it. They want me to tell them how to fix someone. They think I am insinuating that they need help. They are wrong; I never insinuate. I just say it directly.

Instead of caring *for* someone, they have tried to take care *of* them. All too often what many parents call showing care for their children is really doing for them what they need to learn to do for themselves, protecting them from making mistakes or feeling pain, and making them line up in nice straight rows. It makes the children dependent on their parents, communicates that they are not capable, and it is as rejecting as no involvement whatsoever.

The parents are taking care *of* their children, and in doing so, they shame them. When it comes to efforts to take care of a chemically dependent person, family members' attempts to show care to a person who does not think he needs, nor does he want, anyone to care for him, deplete their emotional and psychological resources and shake their spiritual foundation. It is good when their spiritual foundation is shaken, because it has been idolatrous.

The Performance of Others Cannot Overcome Your Shame

The presence of the last ingredient, shame, makes this problem even more difficult. Shame is reinforced and manifests itself in many ways. The presence of shame means that caring has been done for the wrong purpose: to erase the shame of the one doing the caring.

If *I can get my kids to turn out right*, then *I'll feel like a worthwhile parent*. If *I can get my husband or wife to look and act like he/she should*, then *I will know I am a good spouse*. If *I can get that couple in my congregation to straighten up their marriage*, then *I'll be the kind of pastor I was taught I am supposed to be*. This is why family members develop survival roles to try to overcome their shame for not being able to do everything they think they have to do in order to be worthwhile persons.

To say it as clearly as possible, all attempts of family members to fix their dependent loved one are really for the purpose of fixing themselves. Their loved one has become their source of value and well-being, so they strive to turn that person into a good source.

Unable to Fix Her "God"

I remember an occasion when a Christian woman came in my office and shared about her husband's drinking problem, his unfaithfulness, and the pain she felt in the marriage. Her husband had become her god. When he was doing well, she was doing well. When he was a mess, she was a mess. I asked the question, "What are you going to do to be a healthy person whether your husband gets better or not?"

She was insulted. She said, "I'm not the problem; my husband is the problem. If he would get better, I would be just fine!"

Her reply proved that her husband had become her god. She was right in the sense that she was not her husband's problem. He was his problem. She was wrong in the sense that he was her problem. She was her problem.

She continued to state her case by telling me how often and how hard she was praying for him and all of the submission formulas she was following in order to win him to God. These included pretending to agree with things on the outside that she knew on the inside were wrong, or being romantic with him on the outside while feeling disgust toward him on the inside.

There are many teachers and counselors around, Christian and non-Christian alike, who encourage this in the name of submission. The Bible calls it lying. She concluded by saying that she was sure God would not let her down. When she finished, I pointed out that her husband, not God, was her source of well-being. She had a false god, and a drunken, unfaithful one at that. Her spiritual foundation had been shaken. Not only that, but she was asking God to turn her bad false god into a good false god. What made her think that God would want to repair her substitute for Him?

Cling to Grace-full Interaction

In dealing with shame and working toward health in families, a distinction between a law-full and grace-full approach needs to be made and kept very clear. The *law-full* approach affirms coming to a place of value by doing or not doing certain things. This is the approach of the secular world. It is also the approach of legalistic families and churches. It holds out a prize that can never be won. The *grace-full* approach affirms doing or not doing certain things coming from a place of value. In this approach, the gospel offers life and worth as a gift and exhorts behavior that is consistent with the value that is already there because of what God has done.

The *only* helpful approach to shame is a grace-full approach. If you try to approach shame from a law-full stance, you only create more shame, which is what the Law is supposed to create. Only in the context of grace-full relationships with Christ and others can individuals and families find the rest and strength to confront the behavior and relationship problems that otherwise would have indicted them.

The Family System Is Affected

Remember the family in chapter 4 that had become psycho-emotionally and functionally reactive? At one time it may have been healthy. But as the individual members continually tried to overcome their shame and accommodate the presence of an unhealthy and painful situation, the family itself adjusted and began to look very different.

Obviously, then, the goal is to help the family once again operate in a healthy way.

Restoring a Family System to Health

Some general principles are helpful to remember as we begin to discover ways to restore a family to health. They are:

1. Just as the chemically dependent person is powerless to will himself out of his use of the chemicals to which he is addicted, so too is the codependent person powerless to change the chemically dependent person to whom he or she is addicted.

2. If the family as a whole, or individuals in it, are reluctant to seek help, if they continue to ignore their own health, if they continue to act as if they can somehow find a way to control their chemically dependent loved one's addiction or behavior, then the dependency has not gotten painful enough for them yet. It needs to get worse.

3. Families get well one person at a time.
4. The best way to confront the dysfunctional system of which you are a member is to become and stay functional.
5. Saying there is a problem when there is one does not cause the problem; it only exposes it.
6. It is OK to stop supporting things on the outside that you do not support on the inside. This is being honest.
7. For a family to begin to function in a healthy way is necessary and possible, even if the chemically dependent person refuses to be involved.
8. Recovery is a process in the same way that becoming dysfunctional is a process.
9. Codependent people are not so *because* of the chemically dependent person. They are codependent because in their attempts to help the dependent person, they have neglected their own health and have become dependent upon the dependent person as their source of well-being.
10. Family members may be in more pain than the dependent person simply because they do not have chemical use to numb it.
11. The most significant underlying issue in codependency is shame.
12. A grace-full, accepting, redemptive environment is most conducive to recovery from codependency.

From Survival to Abundance

Remember from chapter 5 that codependent people acquire different roles to survive a family in which their basic needs are not being met. Unconditional love and acceptance are nonexistent, no sense of specialness or worth is present, and they have grown accustomed to being or feeling alone (some people get so used to this that they can sit in a church building with five hundred people and still be and feel alone).

In response to law-full pressure to change, role-players simply strive to change themselves into different people living up to different expectations in order to feel OK about themselves. That is why role-players need to be set free by grace to become all God has created them to be. Being set free is a matter of discontinuing role-playing, because roles are not needed to acquire value. Value is already present. Of course, outside of a relationship with God through Christ, people are left to generate their own worth (which can never be accomplished). But having received God's grace through faith (not by trying hard to do everything right), a relationship with Christ is present and provides a foundation of abundant life and value upon which to build healthy relationships and confront unhealthy ones.

From Role-Playing to Reality

From a place of value as a gift through Christ, the persons whose job it is to compensate or overfunction are free to stop trying to make sure everyone gets along. They are free to stop making excuses or explaining away the dependent person's behavior. They can discontinue having to protect everyone from the pain and sadness they should be feeling because of living in a dysfunctional family. They can stop smiling when they are sad. They can stop blaming the dependent person for their troubles and take responsibility for their own dishonesty, manipulativeness, and loss of integrity. They are free to rest from offering caring that was not wanted and help that was not helpful.

From that same place of value as a gift through Christ, the performer is free from having to provide the family with a false sense of value. Erasing the family's failures in order to be a worthwhile person is no longer necessary. Doing it right is no longer the source of this person's good assessment of himself or herself. Instead of carrying the weight of the family's worth on his shoulders, now he can go into the ministry or become a doctor or be a musician or a mechanic because that is most consistent with who God made him to be. Achievement ceases to be a means to acquire esteem. Instead, esteem is present whether or not there are results. Results are left up to God.

Then there is the rebel—the poor, tired rebel. With value from Christ, being compared to the performer (who may, by the way, no longer be performing) no longer carries the weight and meaning it used to. The rebel no longer has anything to prove or assert. Worth is established and secure in Jesus. Acquiring attention by inappropriate behavior is no longer necessary. They are now free to rebel for the right reasons.

There was a man in my church who was viewed by most people as a rebel. He had come from an extremely unhealthy family. He had a history of drug and alcohol use. He became a Christian, found Christian friends, attended a Christian college, married a Christian woman, and attended a Christian church. But basically he was a rebel. His Christian friends told him to comply. The Christian college told him to comply. His Christian wife and Christian in-laws told him to comply. His Christian church told him to comply. He complied as long as he could, then went back to business as usual, which was rebelling. He cut off his church connections, went back to drug and alcohol use, and became sexually immoral. The few times he did show up in church, he acted like he felt out of place and asked questions in ways that pushed people into corners.

After a series of crises, he came to a place where he was willing to seek counseling, so he came to me. He looked defiant, sat defensively, talked sarcastically. I said, "You are really a rebellious person, aren't you?"

"Yeah, what's it to you?" he answered.

"Well," I said, "I was just wondering what's keeping you from rebelling *for* Jesus." This was a new idea to him. "Jesus needs rebellious people, you know. I think you need to be the best rebellious person Jesus ever made."

He had been rebelling against the barrage of messages that said he had to be someone other than who he was in order to be an OK person. The realization that in Christ he was already an OK person set him free to be who he was already for Jesus. He was now free to rebel for the right reasons.

Because worth is a gift from God, received by faith, tension in the family can be faced. Family tension no longer has to be covered up by joking or escaping through television, video games, avoiding home, keeping busy, collecting things, or whatever positive or negative things people do to avoid feeling as much pain as they do.

Grace-full relationships with Christ and others break the cycle of shame. They present an alternative to denial, blaming, and escape as the methods of dealing with painful reality. They provide an environment in which dependent and co-dependent people can acquire healthy living skills and learn to confront instead of accommodate unhealthy behavior. What now passes down through the generations is health, fullness, and an awareness of the need for a radical dependency on Jesus Christ only as the source of value and meaning in life.

11

The Church's Stance: Helpful or Hurtful?

The focus of my remaining two chapters is on the body of Christ. In this chapter, I would like to examine and confront the church as a resource that has often *not* been helpful to those individuals and families who struggle with the problems of chemical dependency. Two phrases, actually, characterize the ways in which the body of Christ has not been helpful. They are *lack of involvement* and *unhelpful help*. In the final chapter, I will discuss the body of Christ in terms of the awesome potential present for help and healing of people in pain.

In this chapter I will discuss three main points: lack of involvement by the church in supporting those with the problem; ways in which the church has, in some cases, actually perpetuated the problem by offering unhelpful help; and answers as to why the church has been uninvolved or involved in unhelpful ways.

Not a Stranger to Churches

I attended church regularly with my family until graduating from high school. Upon going to college, my church attendance gradually diminished and eventually stopped altogether. For a period of a couple of years, I stayed away from church settings completely. After burning out of the fast lane of life (and several colleges), I began attending a Christian college and resumed my church attendance. Upon graduation from college, I entered seminary and continued to attend a church. I had my field education ministry in a large church with multiple staff and a strong social thrust. Upon completion of the internship, my wife and I attended several churches in an attempt to find one in which we could serve and be fed.

Just before my senior year of seminary, I took a position as counselor at a secular inpatient chemical dependency treatment center. By then we had found a church that we considered our home. As graduation from seminary approached, I sensed that I would not be serving in a local church pulpit, as it was clear to me that I had found in counseling the ministry for which I was created. However, even though I was not pastoring a church, my family and I were active in one.

A Lack of Involvement

Two disturbing observations can be made as I look back on my illustrious career as a church attender (someone raised, trained, and currently active in the church community). My first observation is that I was not prepared by the Christian community to understand or to provide meaningful ministry to chemically dependent people or their family members.

I had grown up in church. I graduated from a Christian liberal arts college, the stated goal of which was to prepare young people for lives of ministry. I graduated from a Christian seminary, the stated goal of which was to prepare people for lives of ministry. Yet the extent of exposure I had to the issues of chemical dependency and codependency consisted of one quarter-long survey class in seminary. That class was the only acknowledgment I had seen by the Christian community that the problem of chemical dependency even existed, the only time alcoholics were discussed with compassion, and, in fact, the only hint I had at all that whole families could be disrupted by one person's use of chemicals.

Perhaps in its zeal to minister to the chemically dependent family, the evangelical community had provided opportunities galore to learn how to help. Had I simply slipped through the cracks? I think not. The opportunities to be trained in these issues were simply not available. Even to this day, the attitude in the Christian community that this is our issue is the exception and not the rule.

My second observation leaves me with an equally unpleasant taste. I had not observed any chemically dependent people or their family members finding health in any of the churches I attended. The disappointment of this realization was compounded by the fact that I saw chemically dependent individuals and families find health and restoration, even a relationship with Christ, in secular treatment centers.

Loss of Perspective?

There is rejoicing when a Christian sister who has been unemployed for a long time finally gets a job, or when a brother who has had sickness or an operation is released from the hospital. Why, there is even rejoicing when we get new Bibles for the pews. When the new wallpaper is put up in the sanctuary, when we are able to afford resurfacing the parking lot, when we beat the neighboring church in a Sunday school contest and get a visit from the district superintendent are all times of rejoicing. I guess it must be easier to rejoice over some external sign from which we can gain people's positive opinion of us than it is to rejoice when someone recovers from a problem we have been denying in order to protect people's positive opinions of us.

With the estimated number of alcoholics in our country ranging between ten and thirty million, and with four or five other people affected by every one (these statistics do not include those individuals and families affected by drugs other than alcohol), there is the potential here for some significant ministry.

Not the Church's Issue

I am sure there are many "good" reasons why dependency is not a church issue. After all, many other organizations specialize in these types of problems. They are budgeted and trained for it. Let our people go there (as long as it does not affect their church attendance, giving patterns, or theology).

Then there is the fact that there simply are ministry priorities that are higher on the list of things we need to be concerned about. What would happen if we spent Sunday school time educating families about the effects of drinking on driving, the nature of dependency and codependency, how to and how not to help dependents and codependents, resources available that offer counseling, literature available, or the ways in which shame is reinforced in families. Where would we put our units on "How to Handle Your Bank Account in a Christian Manner" or "Ten Principles for Discovering a Christian Hobby"?

There are many ways we might attempt to motivate involvement on the part of uninvolved people. We may be tempted to shame people into action by reminding them of what they owe God for what He has done for them. We might try to program involvement, much the same way as we program giving, attendance, or witnessing. We might launch an attack against not being involved by presenting our case for involvement based on facts, figures, statistics, and even biblical proof texts. Yet all of these solutions fail to address the real issues and will result in a flurry of short-lived activity at best.

Examples of Unhelpful Help

In spite of our good intentions and high call, the body of Christ has offered much help to the chemically dependent that has not helped. In fact, in some cases we have helped perpetuate the problem. There are many areas in which I have seen this happen. I will mention just three of them.

Our zeal to protect people from pain and problems, combined with our lack of information and misinformation concerning the subjects of use, abuse, and dependency, have resulted in unhelpful education and prevention efforts. The story of prevention strategies in the church is a sad one indeed. We have shamed people out of their behavior patterns, encouraging them to earn God's favor by adhering to certain external codes of behavior. Homes and churches have been transformed into environments where only "spiritual" (happy, pleasant, victorious) feelings and issues can be discussed. Some legalistic, some self-righteous, some misinformed people in places of authority have promoted unscriptural attitudes and stereotypes concerning chemicals and people who use them. Overzealous fellow Christians have made it their personal mission to "fix" problems and pain whenever they see them. Others, shamed by their unsuccessful efforts to change unhealthy family members, barge into other relationships where they are not invited with advice that is not solicited.

In addition, members of our families and churches, young and old alike, have been presented with inaccurate, exaggerated views of the effects of alcohol and drug use. Consequently, we have become guilty of overkill and have lost credibility in the eyes of the world, our kids, and people who want help. You may think the presence of these last two statements strange in a book designed to expose the harmful effects of chemical use. I will share the following illustration in order to clarify my point.

Losing Credibility

A few years ago, I was asked to present a seminar on drug use at a statewide youth discipleship weekend for a certain denomination. During a time when the entire group was assembled together, a slide show was presented to the teenagers. By and large it was an excellent show. The narration and music were relevant to the slides and to the needs of those present. Two-thirds of the way through, a slide appeared with an empty six-pack of a popular brand of beer lying by the side of the road. Next came a picture of a police squad car with blue lights flashing. Sirens blazed on the tape. The next set of slides was comprised, first, of a greasy-haired, stereotype junkie. He was in a filthy room, he had a spaced-out look in his eyes, an empty spoon and candle lay on the table, and he was popping a vein in his arm with a syringe. This was followed by a slide of a graveyard with row upon row of tombstones. Appropriate music accompanied on the soundtrack.

This presentation was unhelpful help. The truth is that you can get busted for drinking a beer when you are a teenager. However, I would venture to say that 99 percent of the teenagers present knew people who had used beer, the vast majority of whom had not been busted. What about those present who had used and not been busted? What about after they reach the legal drinking age? What are we going to scare them with then? The truth is that if the junkie keeps using heroin, eventually he will reach the graveyard. But in the meantime he is about to feel the best he has felt in a long while. What about all those who seem to beat the system and look like they are having the time of their lives?

An even more disturbing question is this: If, in our safe, sterile families and churches, we have teenagers whose minds are so impressionable, whose own beliefs and values are so negotiable that we can cause them to stay away from alcohol and drugs with exaggerations, lies, and scare tactics, what will happen when they find themselves in another environment more expert and comfortable in the use of fear and deception?

Simplistic Solutions Ignore the Facts

In addition to unhelpful education and prevention techniques, there is the area of unhelpful solutions after the problem is present. The reason many of the solutions offered by the church are so unhelpful is that they are simplistic. One of the most simplistic solutions to chemical dependency is abstinence. If the church and families can get the chemically dependent person to quit using, we believe that the problem will be over. This solution betrays a gross ignorance of the nature of chemical dependency, an underestimation of the spiritual, emotional, psychological, and physical ramifications of dependency on the individual, and a lack of awareness of the needs and pain of loved ones. Abstinence is not enough.

Another simplistic, unhelpful solution to the problem offered by the church is involving chemically dependent individuals and their families in the search for the cause. The cause with which the religious community is most enamored is sin. I fear that the goal of this approach is to label alcohol use as sin and cause avoidance of alcohol use by encouraging avoidance of sin.

First, abstinence is inadequate as a solution to chemical dependency. Second, while the abuse of and/or addiction to chemicals indicates the presence of sin in the life of the dependent person, the New Testament does not label the use of alcohol as a sin.

There have been, and will continue to be, attempts in the religious community to say that the wine in the New Testament was not alcoholic. This line of reasoning ignores the cultural context of the New Testament. Among other things, it makes Paul's advice to Timothy in 1 Timothy 5:23 meaningless, it makes Peter's statement in Acts 2:15 senseless, and it suggests that Jesus' water-to-wine miracle in John 2 took place in a legalistic Bible college in the twentieth century, rather than in a culture where the poor wine was saved until the wedding guests were too intoxicated to notice its lack of quality. And in Ephesians 5:18, what is the sense of exhorting the Ephesians to refrain from getting drunk from wine that could not get them drunk in the first place?

How Can We Help vs. How Did This Happen?

My purpose has not been to minimize the presence or ravages of sin. The sin involved in chemical dependency is every bit as destructive as it is for someone who is overweight, breaks the speed limit, feels superior to other people because of his own performance, cheats on his income tax, or rapes someone. I have simply desired to point out the inadequacy and futility of solving the problem by figuring out the cause.

Phil Edwards, a great friend who is an urban ministries expert on the mission field in Kenya, gave me the following illustration one day while voicing his frustration concerning this approach. He said that the way the church tries to solve the problem of chemical dependency can be compared to a parent who looks through the living room window and sees that his beloved child who, because of playing on the street, has been run over by a hit-and-run driver. Upon reaching the scene of the accident, he finds the child barely conscious. He picks up the child in his arms and says to a bystander, "Why was my child playing on the street after I told her not to? Do you think it was because of peer pressure? Do you think it was an accident or willful disobedience? Is it because my child is such a sinner?"

My answer to the parent's questions is "Who cares?" Now is not the time to worry about how it happened. Now is the time to take emergency action by getting the child to people who specialize in helping those who have been run over in traffic accidents. The same is true when we find addicts and codependents. They need the help of trained specialists, not self-appointed spiritual monitors. While self-righteous people in the church are asserting their rightness, individuals and families are dying. Do you know what? In the time it has taken you to read this illustration, two people have been killed by drunk drivers. I wonder how many addicts and codependents have sunk deeper into their problems because fingers have been pointed instead of helping hands offered.

Good-Intentioned Samaritans

The final example of unhelpful help lies in the area of unhelpful relationships. I have gone into great detail in chapters 4, 5, and 7 describing the behaviors and attitudes of family members that actually perpetuate the problem. Rather than go over old ground, I wish at this point to give some examples of how those relationships look in church settings. For example, pastors who diagnose every problem as something they have been trained to help, namely, spiritual problems, miss opportunities to offer ministry to many other needs of the person. I am no longer able to count the number of times that I have seen individuals and families begin to get better when the pastor who was helping began helping them for the right problem, or when people sought help outside the church because their pastor or fellow church members were inflexible and would not abandon their unhelpful course of action.

Talking the spouse into returning home because the alcoholic has convinced the pastor that he/she will try harder is not helpful. Paying bills, bailing out of jail, and pleading for the person's job are not helpful actions. Anything that stands in the way of persons experiencing the natural consequences of their own behavior is not helpful. Encouragement to try harder to follow systems or formulas is not helpful. It is asking an out-of-control person to be in control. Asking family members questions to which you already know the answers is not helpful. Praying that God will keep the person from getting into trouble is not helpful. Pray, instead, that God will bring as much trouble into the person's life as it will take to convince him that his life is failing and he is needy.

A Distinction That Is False

There are many reasons why churches have been uninvolved in people's pain or involved in ways that have not been helpful. Some of them are easier to understand than others. For instance, I have noticed an alarming trend in the religious community in general, and in many pastors specifically, to accentuate the distinction between secular turf and holy turf, as if God is not the God of everything. We do this with our approach to public vs. Christian schools. We do it again with our emphasis on the separation of church and state. We do it, once more, when it comes to the needs and problems of people.

A prevalent view is that the church is the place for spiritual problems, not those that are emotional or psychological in nature. This view impales us on the horns of a dilemma. When an emotional or psychological problem surfaces, we must either trust the secular community to help the person with the problem (except we do not trust the secular community), or rediagnose everything to be something we have been trained to help (which, we have just discovered, isn't helpful).

I have noticed, too, in churches that hold strongly to this distinction that there is very little sharing of even spiritual problems. Spiritual problems are shared usually only after they have been overcome, for the purpose of instructing others, and not often during the struggle for the purpose of asking for help.

Yet to simply say that if the body of Christ cared about whole persons—all of their needs, all of their relationships—the problem would be solved is simply one more of many simplistic, superficial solutions to the deep, complicated problems of human pain and family dysfunction. There are two awful truths underlying lack of involvement and unhelpful help on the part of the body of Christ. These truths are of eternal significance and cannot be taken lightly.

When the Church Is Not the Body

The first thing that might explain the kind of involvement the body of Christ has or has not had in helping people with chemical dependency and other kinds of issues is that what we have come to view as the body of Christ is not really the body at all. The organized church and the body of Christ are not one and the same. The body of Christ is a living organism, united and energized by the Spirit of God. The church is an organization. An organized church is incorporated in the state where it is located, exempt from federal and state income tax, and state sales and usage tax. We call it a Christian organization because it adheres to Christian principles, promotes Christian doctrines, supports Christian endeavors, and tries not to allow non-Christians to belong or vote.

However, there is no such thing as a Christian organization. Only living things can be Christian. Since when did calling oneself something, adhering to something, promoting something, supporting something, meeting in a certain location, or excluding someone make anyone Christian? Receiving life and forgiveness as a gift, by faith, on the basis of what God accomplished through Christ is what makes someone a Christian. Being transformed into a new creation by the work of God's Spirit is what makes someone a Christian, not adhering to a certain set of rules, or assenting to certain beliefs, or receiving a certain label.

In Matthew 7:21–23, Jesus said:

> Not everyone who says to Me, "Lord, Lord," shall enter the kingdom of heaven, but he who does the will of My Father in heaven. Many will say to Me in that day, "Lord, Lord, have we not prophesied in Your name, cast out demons in Your name, and done many wonders in Your name?" And then I will declare to them, "I never knew you; depart from Me, you who practice lawlessness!"

I realize that this passage is not specifically about the church. But it is about some people who thought they belonged to Jesus because of the good, beneficial, even supernatural things they did in the name of Jesus, lawless people who did lawful things. The thing that disturbs me about this passage is that Jesus uses the word *many* to describe them. He also uses the word *many* to describe those who enter the wide gate that leads to destruction (v. 13) as opposed to the few who find life through the narrow gate (v. 14).

Who are the many and who are the few? I think it is grandiose and naïve to think that the few are in the church building, our church building, on Sunday morning, while the many are in bed or playing golf or watching TV. Could it be that the many and the few are in the same building on Sunday morning? What could be the reason that there is so little care, support, grace, forgiveness, fellowship, comfort, bearing of burdens, and encouraging in so many churches? Could it possibly be that those churches are simply made up of the *many*, in whom there is no life, from whom there can be no fruit, and the *few*, who are already producing what fruit there is out of fullness and love, without guilt trips or programs?

These questions are difficult, but they need to be raised. Are we spending our time pep-talking dead trees to produce fruit when we should be doing the work of the evangelist? "Every good tree bears good fruit" (Matt. 7:17) is Jesus' description of the truth, not His plea for the dead trees to produce fruit. "You will know them by their fruits" (Matt. 7:16) is Jesus' method for determining if there is life, not an exhortation to produce activity where there is no life. Does the body of Christ have to be coerced into acting like the body, created by programs and positive self-effort, or can you see it functioning if you simply watch from whom the fruit comes?

This raises another frightening question. Could the *many/few* explain the preoccupation of many churches, denominations, and Christian colleges with performance, how things look, and creating and protecting turfs that can be seen, such as buildings, parking lots, increased giving or attendance figures, or the way our kids turn out? I thought that the focus of the Christian and the body of Christ is on what cannot be seen or touched—on things above. We walk by faith, not by sight. What explains the loss of focus? One explanation might be that a person or church focuses on the natural, temporal things because that is all they have. When this is true, it is again needful to do the work of the evangelist. It is possible that what we have thought was a living organism, melted together by the Holy Spirit, was only a religious organization, frozen together by corporate bylaws, doctrine, or common turf.

When the Body Becomes a Codependent System

Another reason for lack of involvement or unhelpful help on the part of the body of Christ might be the presence of the second awful truth. The body of Christ is a system just like a family, made up of individual, interrelated, interdependent parts. The body of Christ might have become sick and dysfunctional just like the families I have described. In fact, it might have been sick already from any number of issues that were never dealt with. In Galatians 5:1–15, Paul exhorted the body to expel the leaven of legalism so the whole would not be affected. And in 1 Corinthians 5:6–8, Paul told the body to remove the leaven of immorality specifically, and the leaven of self-pride in general, so the whole could again be as clean as Christ created it.

Much of what we're looking at refers to individuals and family members. It can also be applied to a hurting family and the other families that are in the body, or to the hurting individual and others in the body.

When relationships function this way in a church, the body of Christ there is not helpful because it cannot be. It is too sick itself. Like families, entire church systems can adjust to accommodate and maintain the unhealth of their members.

How the Body of Christ Becomes Dysfunctional

Recall the three ingredients discussed in chapter 4 that need to be present for an individual to be affected. First, you have to care. The degree to which a loved one's chemical dependency can harm you depends upon the second ingredient, unawareness or ill-awareness. Ingredient three, the presence of shame, compounds the situation even more. When these three ingredients are present in the body of Christ, it will become a codependent system like the family systems described in previous chapters. The result is a system that cannot get better or help others because it is drawing life and value from something other than its true source, the Spirit of God.

I am going to assume that the fact that you are reading this book in the first place means you care and are sensing the need to become more aware of the subject. Hence, the first two ingredients are present in you, so I am going to concentrate on the phenomenon of shame in the body of Christ.

Remember the definition of shame? Shame is the painful feeling of being bad as a person, of being defective, inadequate, of lacking value. The purpose of God's law is to drive human beings to that assessment of themselves based on their inadequate performance. But the fulfillment of the Law is a relationship with Christ, right-standing with God, and a new self-assessment based on Christ's more than adequate performance. The presence of shame (a negative self-assessment based on performance) indicates one of two things.

First, the person has not been driven to Christ, is not under grace but condemnation, and his shameful self-assessment is accurate. He needs to receive life. Please do not pep-talk this person to produce fruit; he might end up teaching your kids in Sunday school.

Second, after having received forgiveness and a new identity as a gift on the basis of Christ's performance on the cross, he has never been taught to continue walking in Christ in the same way he came. He was never reminded or discipled to continue focusing on Christ only as his source of life, value, and identity. Hence, he has begun once again to judge himself by his own performance. Consequently, he is either feeling ashamed because of his inadequate performance, self-righteous because of his successful performance, or too paralyzed to try for fear of failing or even making a mistake.

Trying to Earn What We Already Have

Instead of giving *ourselves* to people who are having problems, we give pat answers, formula Bible verses, and casseroles. We do not know how gifted and adequate we are in Christ. This is why there are so many uninvolved, inactive Christians in the body. I call them secret agent Christians—people who spend their whole lives trying to be someone other than who they are for God. Their plan is that when they get this quality, or get rid of that one, *then* they will be fit for God's service. They do not realize that *then* is already here because of what God has done in them.

We feel uncomfortable around the pain of others and try to squeeze them into our pattern. Instead of being safe in Christ, we seek safety in our similarity to others. Often, for the lack of the right answer for someone's problems, we avoid them instead of placing an arm around them or giving them a hug. We are measuring our spirituality by how together we are, which is why we want things to look good even if we have to deny our real feelings, impressions, and opinions. We are seeking to please people and gain acceptance, having forgotten that we already please God by virtue of being in His Son, that our acceptance has been bought on the cross and sealed by God's own Spirit.

Actually, the best Satan (the Accuser) can do to sterilize and neutralize persons who are new, who have life, who are gifted and valuable, and in whom the very Spirit of God dwells, is to indict them and convince them to set off on a lifelong course of trying to acquire with their own performance what they already have because of Christ's performance. Like dogs chasing their tails, many Christians sit in the same place, never going forward or even backward. They never use the power or give away the grace they have received because their perception is that they do not have it yet.

12

"Grace-full" Relationships:
The Environment Needed for Health

Does chemical dependency occur in "good" Christian homes, schools, and churches? Does it affect more than the person using the chemical? Should the goal of those trying to help be more than simply abstinence on the part of the dependent person? Is involving loved ones in the process of their own recovery necessary? Is there opportunity for ministry here? My hope is that after having read chapters 1 through 11, your answer to all of these questions is a resounding yes!

Several concepts found in the Bible affirm our interrelatedness and interdependence, underscore the necessity to confront and support dysfunctional fellow members, and demonstrate the potential and responsibility of the body of Christ to bring a message of good news for chemically dependent persons and those who love them. This final chapter addresses the involvement of the church in the recovery of chemically dependent individuals and codependent families. Three main points are addressed: the need to help, the potential to help, and how to help.

A System That Needs to Stay Healthy

This first section represents a theology of church involvement. It answers the question, "Why does the church need to be involved in helping chemically dependent persons and those who love them?" Many factors demonstrate that constructive involvement on the part of the body of Christ is absolutely vital, even inescapable. All of these have to do with the fact that the body of Christ is a system.

In chapter 11, I suggested that one explanation for the lack of involvement on the part of the body of Christ in helping members who are experiencing difficulties is that, like the families described in chapters 4 and 5, it, too, has grown dysfunctional. Because of its nature as a system, the body of Christ must provide the health input and relationships that God intended. The health of the members depends, to a great degree, on the health of the system of which they are a part. And the health of the entire system depends, to a great degree, on the health of the members who comprise it.

More Than a Sermon Illustration

Body of Christ itself is one of the system concepts found in the Scriptures. Not simply a metaphor or sermon illustration, "body of Christ" is the magnificent way in which the apostle Paul described the supernatural interrelatedness of people who have a relationship with Jesus Christ. In Romans 12:4–5, Paul said, "For as we have many members in one body, but all the members do not have the same function, so we, being many, are one body in Christ, and individually members of one another." In 1 Corinthians 6:15, he said, "Do you not know that your (*plural*) bodies (*plural*) are members (*plural*) of Christ (*singular*)?" (italics mine). Paul did not even say "members of Christ's body" in this text, but rather "members of Christ" no less! This sounds a little more supernatural than a sermon illustration, doesn't it?

First Corinthians 12:12 says, "For as the body is one and has many members, but all the members of that one body, being many, are one body, so also is Christ." Again, Paul used nothing less than "Christ" as the summary of the members of the body. And in verse 27 of the same chapter we see the same thing, "Now you (*plural*) are the body (*singular*) of Christ, and members individually" (italics mine). We are members of a system, like it or not.

Not only is the nature of our relationship with one another supernatural, but the cause of our relationship with one another is supernatural, as well. First Corinthians 12:13 says, "For by one Spirit we (*plural*) were all (*plural*) baptized into one body (*singular*)." Compare this to joining a local church that may involve our application, testimony, examination, and/or attendance at new members' classes, or a vote of acceptance by the congregation or governing body of the corporation.

"We were baptized" is an aorist, passive in the Greek, which means that being baptized into the body of Christ is a one-point-in-time accomplished act done to us and not by us. In verse 18 we read, "But now God has set the members, each one of them, in the body just as He pleased." We are not members of the same system by virtue of having chosen it, but by virtue of having been chosen for it.

Membership in the church corporation is required in order to vote on corporate business issues, serve as an officer of the corporation, or represent the corporation at denominational functions. As a member of the corporation, a person could choose not to be involved in these corporate activities, which may or may not have an effect on the other members of the corporation. But when it comes to the body of Christ, what one member does or experiences *does* affect the other members. First Corinthians 5:6 says, "Do you not know that a little leaven leavens the whole lump?" The Scripture does not say a little leaven *could* leaven the lump.

The same concept can be found in the different context of 1 Corinthians 12:26, "And if one member suffers, all the members suffer with it; or if one member is honored, all the members rejoice with it." The Scripture does not say if one member suffers, all *should* suffer, and if one is honored, all *should* rejoice. By virtue of being members of the same system (body), our lives affect and are affected by one another. This is not optional.

Fellowship Is Not Optional

Other concepts in Scripture illustrate the system of which Christians are a part. One such concept is that of *fellowship*. A word study of the Greek word *koinonia*, the word translated "fellowship," will reveal that fellowship means participation in something with someone. Fellowship is more than showing up at the same place and time as someone else; more than believing in the same thing, saying the same clichés, looking the same, promoting the same programs. Again, something supernatural is happening here.

For instance, 1 John 1:3 says, "And truly our fellowship is with the Father and with His Son Jesus Christ. " In 2 Corinthians 6:14, Paul asked the rhetorical question, "And what communion [fellowship] has light with darkness?" The answer is none! First John 1:5–6 explains, "God is light and in Him is no darkness at all. If we say that we have fellowship with Him, and walk in darkness, we lie and do not practice the truth." The Bible also says that Christians fellowship with the Lord Jesus (1 Cor. 1:9). To fellowship with Him in His life, suffering, death, burial, resurrection, and victory means more than deciding to accept those phenomena as fact, or agreeing that what He did was a good idea. Fellowship means participating in them with Him. First John 1:7 says, "But if we walk in the light as He is in the light, we have fellowship with one another."

"Walking in the light" with one another is John's explanation of the origin of our relationship with other Christians. Therefore, if a *fellow* family member, *fellow* church member, *fellow* heir, *fellow* citizen, *fellow* partaker of the promises, is in fellowship with darkness (in this case the delusion and dysfunction of chemical dependency or codependency), the fellowship between that person and God, His Son, and other Christians is profoundly affected. Relationships are about light or darkness.

Chasing Chemicals Instead of Building the Body

Another passage that addresses the importance of a healthy body of believers is Ephesians 4:14–16. The Scripture begins with the word "that," which means literally "in order that." Something is true "in order that" something else can happen. What has happened?

> There is one body and one Spirit. . . . and [Christ] gave gifts to men. . . . for equipping of the saints for the work of ministry, for the edifying of the body of Christ . . . that we should no longer be children, tossed to and fro and carried about with every wind of doctrine, by the trickery of men, in the cunning craftiness by which they lie in wait to deceive, but, speaking the truth in love, may grow up in all things into Him who is the head—Christ—from whom the whole body, joined and knit together by what every joint supplies, according to the effective working by which every part does its share, causes

growth of the body for the edifying of itself in love (Eph. 4:4, 8, 12, 14–16).

The truth of the matter is that chemically dependent members of the body of Christ are pouring their time, energy, emotions, their very life into a relationship with chemicals. They are not capable of supplying that which fits and holds together the body, for they are not an individual part that is working properly. This can also be said about those codependent family members and others who love the chemically dependent person and have sought to derive their sense of peace and value from their dependent loved one. Preoccupation with the problems of the dependent person, the wasted investment of time, energy, and emotions to fix them, and their seeking to derive their sense of well-being from someone other than God, only result in more dysfunctional members. These members, likewise, are not able to contribute to the building up of the body because they are not working properly and have little left to supply.

The Wonderful "One Anothers"

This brings me to the "one anothers" in the New Testament, which is but one more concept that affirms we are members of a system and need to be involved in helping dysfunctional members. Not including those instances found in the Gospels, the Greek word *allelon*, translated "one another," appears fifty-eight times in the New Testament. *Allelon* is what is known in the Greek language as a reciprocal pronoun, which means that both parties will experience the action of the verb by virtue of both parties providing the action of the verb. For instance, "love one another" means that both will experience being loved by virtue of both doing the loving. "Bear one

another's burdens" means that both will have their burdens
borne by virtue of both bearing burdens. "Comfort one another" means that both will be comforted by virtue of both
doing the comforting.

The "one anothers" in the New Testament communicate
God's intention for us to be involved in each other's lives.
Every "one another" imperative is for the purpose of growing
stronger spiritually as a result of functioning in relationship
with other members of the body of Christ. The foundation of
spiritual maturity is dependence upon God only as the source
of all of life. The foundation develops in deep relationships
growing out of involvement with, openness toward, and interdependence on fellow members of Christ.

God's own Spirit has created, unified, and energized a
system (the body of Christ) custom-made for fostering spiritual growth. That system is undermined and God's provision
short-circuited by uninvolvement, absence of vulnerability,
and lack of honesty (not just dishonesty) on the part of its
members. This is true when these things result from the presence of chemical dependency in one of the members. This is
equally true when they result from an attitude of a member
that his life issues are his own and nobody else's business,
or when a member neglects to seek help and support for any
pain because of reliance upon the opinions of others as a
source of security.

Churches are dysfunctional for many reasons. One of the
reasons is that we have refused to accept chemical dependency,
and other dysfunctions in our members, as our issue.

The Potential to Help

I feel absolutely incapable of expressing in adequate terms
the potential that is the body of Christ's to help chemically

dependent persons and those who love them. What other agency, group, club, or fellowship is the dwelling place of the very Spirit of God? Scripture is rich in its description of the resources that are ours because we have His Spirit, individually and corporately. Let's learn some of what is true about who we are and what we have because we have the Holy Spirit.

During His last hours with the disciples, Jesus shared many things that would be true because of the coming of the Spirit. In John 16:7, Jesus said, "Nevertheless I tell you the truth. It is to your advantage that I go away; for if I do not go away, the Helper will not come to you; but if I depart, I will send Him to you."

What will the coming of the Spirit, the sending of the Helper, mean to those on the receiving end? The answer is in John 14:12. Here Jesus said, "Most assuredly, I say to you, he who believes in Me, the works that I do he will do also; and greater works than these will he do, because I go to My Father." The answer is also in John 16:13: "However, when He, the Spirit of truth, has come, He will guide you into all truth." In Acts 1:8, Jesus said, "But you shall receive power when the Holy Spirit has come upon you." In Ezekiel 37:14, the prophet waited for the day when the Holy Spirit would be put *in* us, not simply upon us. "I will put My Spirit in you, and you shall live."

Still Waiting for the Spirit?

Life? Power? Knowing all truth? Greater works than Jesus? Sure, someday, but only with the coming of the Holy Spirit! Good news! In 2 Corinthians 1:21–22, Paul wrote, "Now He who establishes us with you in Christ and has anointed us is God, who also has sealed us and given us the Spirit in our hearts as a deposit." Romans 8:9 confirms this: "But you are not in the flesh but in the Spirit, if indeed the Spirit of God dwells in you. Now if anyone does not have the Spirit of Christ, he is not His."

Helpful activity that results from our own self-effort as we attempt to live up to some standard is impotent, tiring, and foul-smelling to God. There is, however, helpful activity that is supernatural and does not burn out anyone. This activity results from living in a way that is consistent with the identity that is ours as a gift because of God's effort. This is the difference between being the source of the activity or the channel through which God's activity flows.

Introducing a Better Temple

As a result of the Holy Spirit in our midst, a powerful statement has been made concerning our identity. We are "the temple of God." Paul said in 1 Corinthians 3:16–17:

> Do you not know that you (*plural*) are the temple (*singular*) of God and that the Spirit of God dwells in you (*plural*)? If anyone defiles the temple of God, God will destroy him. For the temple of God is holy, which temple you (*plural*) are.

This Scripture does not say that you, John Doe (*singular*), are God's temple, so do not put cigarette smoke in there because the Holy Spirit has set up a no-smoking zone. There are many, many reasons not to smoke, but to use this, or 1 Corinthians 6:19, as a proof text against smoking, drinking, or overeating is to misuse the text and miss its full impact. First Corinthians 6:19 says, "Or do you not know that your (*plural*) body (*singular*) is the temple (*singular*) of the Holy Spirit who is in you (*plural*)?" The body of Christ, which is not one member but many members, is a temple of God.

What are the ramifications of being members of the body that is a temple of God? The Old Testament temple was a "scary, stay away, you can't come in" sort of place that had areas where only the High Priest could enter. Every year when the priest entered those places, the people of God were reminded that they were not worthy to enter. Nevertheless, God's people saw the temple as the place where He lived. The temple was where a person went to experience God and His forgiveness, cleansing, and redemption.

Under the old covenant, the High Priest was priest of a temple made with hands. He was the minister of sacrifices that could only cover sin. When he finished, he had to leave the place of sacrifice immediately until he returned to make the next sacrifice. The condition of the sinners remained the same. They were still unholy, still in need of future sacrifices, and still unworthy to enter the temple.

> For the law, having a shadow of the good things to come, and not the very image of the things, can never with these same sacrifices, which they offer continually year by year, make those who approach perfect. For then would they not have ceased to be offered? For the worshipers, once purged, would have had no more consciousness of sins. But in those sacrifices there is a reminder of sins every year. . . . And every priest stands ministering daily and offering repeatedly the same sacrifices, which can never take away sins. (Heb. 10:1–3, 11)

With a Better High Priest!

But Hebrews 10 is not finished yet. We have a better High Priest.

By that will we have been sanctified through the offering of the body of Jesus Christ once for all. . . . But this Man, after He had offered one sacrifice for sins forever, sat down at the right hand of God. . . . For by one offering He has perfected forever those who are being sanctified. . . . Now where there is remission of these, there is no longer an offering for sin. Therefore, brethren, having boldness to enter the Holiest by the blood of Jesus . . . let us draw near with a true heart in full assurance of faith, having our hearts sprinkled from an evil conscience and our bodies washed with pure water. (vv. 10, 12, 14, 18, 19, and 22)

The sacrifice of our great High Priest was not some temporary covering of sin. His was a once-for-all (one time for everyone) sacrifice that did not need to be repeated. Our condition after His sacrifice was positively altered. We have been made holy, perfected for all time, in need of no future sacrifices on our behalf ("It is finish!" John 19:30). In addition, we are worthy and encouraged to enter the holy place with confidence (see also Heb. 4:16). Not only are we now worthy to enter the temple over which Jesus Christ is High Priest, but *we are* the temple over which Jesus Christ is High Priest.

Is "the temple that we are" still a "scary, stay away, you can't come in" sort of place? Or is it a place where someone in need of love, forgiveness, cleansing, and even life can come and experience God, the source of these things? I rebuke those who have turned "the temple that we are" into a place where people's pain is of no concern. I rebuke those who have turned "the temple that we are" into a place that seems safe only to those who measure themselves by their lack of external signs of inward pain. "If anyone defiles the temple of God, God will destroy him. For the temple of God is holy, which temple you are" (1 Cor. 3:17).

Taking Seriously Our Christ-Earned Identity

A partial list of other scriptural descriptions of the identity and resources that are ours as a gift because of Christ's performance concludes this section.

Romans 5:1—having been **justified** by faith, we have **peace with God**

5:10—we were **reconciled to God**

6:2—we who **died to sin**

6:6—our **old man** was **crucified**

6:11—**dead to sin**

6:14—**not under law** but **under grace**

7:6—we have been **delivered from the law**

8:1—**no condemnation** to those who are **in Christ Jesus**

8:16—we are **children of God**

1 Corinthians 1:2—those who are **sanctified**

1:5—you were **enriched in everything**

6:11—you were **washed,** you were **sanctified,** you were **justified**

2 Corinthians 2:15—we are to God the **fragrance of Christ**

5:17—a **new creation**

Galatians 3:27—**put on Christ**

3:29—**heirs** according to the promise

4:7—a **son (or daughter)** then an heir

Ephesians 1:3—**blessed** us **with every spiritual blessing**

1:4—**holy** and **without blame** before Him

1:7—we have **redemption, forgiveness** of sins

1:11—we have **obtained an inheritance**

2:5—made **alive**

2:6—**raised** us **up** together, and made us sit together **in heavenly places**

2:10—**His workmanship**

2:13—you have been **made near**

2:19—**fellow citizens** of the household of God

3:6—**fellow heirs**, of the same body, and partakers of His promise

Philippians 1:11—being **filled with the fruits of righteousness**

2:15—you shine as **lights in the world**

Colossians 1:13—**delivered** us **from** the power of **darkness** and **translated** us **into the kingdom**

1:22—**holy**, and **blameless**, and **irreproachable**

2:10—you are **complete** in Him

3:1—**raised with Christ**

3:12—the **elect** of God, **holy** and **beloved**

Hebrews 3:1—**holy brethren**, partakers of the heavenly calling

1 Peter 1:23—**born again**, not of corruptible seed, but of **incorruptible**

2:9—**a chosen generation**, a **royal priesthood**

Did you know that none of what I just listed is based on our performance? These Scriptures are simply a statement of our identity and resources, received as a gift, by faith, made possible by the cross. For the Christian life to be more than an exercise in self-effort in the name of God, we must act by faith in a way that is consistent with who we already are and what we already have because of the performance of a God who is faithful. "And God is able to make *all* grace *abound* toward you, that you, *always* having *all sufficiency* in *all* things, have an *abundance* for *every* good work" (2 Cor. 9:8, italics mine).

On to the list of good works.

Living Consistently Will Help Others

A way that the body of Christ can be a place of good news for chemically dependent persons and those who love them is to believe the good news and its ramifications, and to act as though it is as true as it is. Paul said in Philippians 3:16, "Nevertheless, to the degree that we have already attained, let us walk by the same rule, let us be of the same mind." The previous section described where "we have already attained." We have attained the standard by grace. Practical living is not a matter of trying to earn or attain anything; everything was earned and attained on the cross. Practical living is a matter of living and acting toward one another in a way that is consistent with having already attained the standard.

In Romans 6:1 and 2, Paul urged us to quit sinning (even though our sin allows God, who loves to pour out grace, an opportunity to do so). But the reasoning behind his exhortation to stop sinning was not because sinning is against the Law (even though it is). Neither is it because sinning displeases God (even though it does). These tend to be the two main reasons we tell people not to sin. Paul's reason was that it is totally inconsistent for a "dead to sin" creature to continue in sin! Not sinning is a more consistent manifestation of what it means to be a new creature (see 2 Cor. 5:17), whose old self was crucified (see Rom. 6:6). Therefore, stop acting dead (because you aren't) and start acting alive (because you are)! (See Rom. 6:12.) *That's* the good news!

Doing the "One Anothers" out of Fullness

One of the ways the body of Christ can be very helpful to people is to *do* the "one anothers." I have already talked in previous chapters about what I think it means to agape-love one another and to accept one another. There are some additional "one anothers" that apply specifically to the issue of chemical dependency. These include not lying to one another (Col. 3:9), not speaking against one another (James 4:11), not complaining against one another (James 5:9), forgiving one another (Eph. 4:32), giving preference to one another when it comes to receiving honor (Rom. 12:10), confessing to one another (James 5:16), and admonishing one another (Rom. 15:14; Col. 3:16). There are others, but these are enough to give you the idea.

However, remembering certain principles when approaching the "one anothers" is essential. First, acting in the ways described by the "one anothers" is not simply a matter of deciding to be nicer to people or following a set of rules more conducive to harmony in human relationships. There is a reason why I can love you with no strings—not just if you respond the way I want. There is a reason I can accept you the way you are and not try to turn you into the person I need you to be. I do not have to pretend that you are not really struggling with any problems. There is a reason why I do not have to spread rumors against you or talk behind your back to others.

It is the same reason that I can follow Ephesians 4:25, which says, "Therefore, putting away lying, each one speak truth with his neighbor, for we are members of one another."

When I have a problem with you, I can tell you, and I can include all of the truth. I have no need to con myself into thinking I am honest simply because I have not lied. I do not have to protect myself under the guise of not hurting your feelings, which is treating you as though you cannot handle the truth about yourself.

I can perform those and the remaining "one anothers" because I already have my life, value, and meaning as a gift from God, based upon the cross. I do not have to fix you to be OK. I do not have to make things look good to be OK. Getting credit for something does not make me more complete. Neither does spreading rumors about you to get people on my side. I can forgive you and let go of the thing you did that I now realize cannot devaluate me. I can tell you the truth, even if you do not like me afterward (remember, earned love is not love at all). I can even confess my shortcomings to you, because my perfection is established and secure in Christ, not on the basis of my perfect performance of everything.

The "one anothers" are good works that *result*, not from self-effort or commitment to try harder, but from getting life and value *only* from God. The only works that are truly good are the ones that result from this focus on God as our source. Everything else is just an exercise in religious self-effort.

Many Ways to Say "Have One God!"

The Bible urges us to focus on one God. In Matthew 7:24–25 it is called building our house on the rock. In 1 Corinthians 1:31, Paul said, "He who glories, let him glory in the LORD." In Galatians 2:20, he said, "And the life which I now live in the flesh I live by faith in the Son of God," not by trying hard to follow the rules. Ephesians 4:1 and following tells us the specifics of the Christian life. But the exhortations follow Paul's most incredible prayer in 3:14–21, in which he pleads with God to enable the Ephesians to understand just who they are and what they have in Christ. In Colossians 2:6, Paul said, "As you have therefore received Christ Jesus the Lord, so walk in Him." We are to walk the way we received Him in the first place, not by gritting our teeth and trying to be spiritual, but by faith in Him for our life.

In Philippians 3:1–9, Paul said that even though he had a mind to put confidence in what is natural, he counted everything as rubbish for the surpassing value of knowing Christ Jesus. Verse 9 summarizes, "and be found in Him, not having my own righteousness, which is from the law, but that which is through faith in Christ, the righteousness which is from God by faith. Hebrews 4:9–10 says, "There remains therefore a rest for the people of God. For he who has entered His rest has himself also ceased from his works as God did from His."

In both letters to Timothy, Paul referred to the Christian life as a fight of faith. I think he used the word *fight* because that is what it is. In the midst of all the things we can see, hear, taste, and touch that promise to make us alive, full, or more complete, it is a fight to believe a God we cannot perceive with our physical senses.

Who or what we rest, trust, boast, put confidence, and have faith in are issues that must be settled before we decide what specific programs or activities we will undertake to help those struggling with various problems.

This is about God-based, grace-full environments in which people can experience God in a forgiving, healing, even saving way. Can you imagine what it would be like for a family in the grasp of the darkness and delusion of chemical dependency to be in the midst of a body of believers who walk in the light? No keeping secrets; no pretending not to see what is really there; no acting as though spirituality depends on adherence to certain formulas; no need to hide problems or struggles in order to earn the approval of man. Programs and structure would serve people instead of vice versa. Life and love would be freely received and freely given.

More Practical Suggestions

I have tried to describe the foundation upon which programs and activities can be built. The foundation is not negotiable. Because of the nonnegotiable identity that is ours, the body of Christ can play a very significant part in helping chemically dependent persons and those who love them. I would like to close with some very negotiable suggestions for activities and programs that begin to address the issue of chemical dependency in the local church.

Hardly a place in the community has the opportunity to address the issue of chemical dependency with as much potential as the body of Christ. Few people, for instance, have as much potential for impact as a pastor who preaches grace and is well informed about the dynamics of dysfunctional relationships. I know of only one professional, the pastor, who is expected to make personal visits to the homes of the people on his or her caseload. A pastor can often knock on someone's door and walk into the house without so much as a call on the telephone.

What if that pastor had learned how to pick up on some of the ways chemically dependent people and family members ask for help? What if he could refer that family to two or three resources in the community? Suppose he could suggest helpful books, pamphlets, or tapes? I cannot emphasize enough the need for every pastor to receive formal training in the area of family systems and in preventing and diagnosing those problems that cause entire systems to become dysfunctional.

All week long, many professionals in society perceive people as having the problems they have been trained to treat. This gives them purpose and funnels insurance money in their direction. A Sunday morning sermon, evening seminar, or Sunday school class may be the only times all week when teachers, lawyers, judges, doctors, social workers, and psychologists all meet together in one room without having to be right about issues.

There is no need for people who get life and security from Jesus to diagnose a problem in a way that will bring the treatment dollar into their area of expertise. What an opportunity to give all of them the same information about chemical dependency and codependency. What an opportunity to network with other Christian professions. This does not even include the benefits to individuals and families who need the information, or who need to talk to Christian professionals who have an understanding of people's pain.

Recently, our church offered four Sunday evening sessions entitled "Breaking the Silence: Beginning to Deal with Tough Issues." Experts on the subjects presented sessions on communicating about touchy issues, protecting children from sexual abuse, family violence, and shame. People who were struggling in those areas shared their struggles. Not only did this series give valuable information to professionals and laypeople, in addition it gave people the message that these issues are *our* issues. The series also gave individuals and families permission to ask for help and support for problems "we don't have here." Woven throughout the entire series was the message that problems (or lack of problems) are not a measure of spirituality; we are who we are because of Christ. Needless to say, many people have received help as a result of experiencing the grace to ask for it.

Few, if any, organizations have property that is utilized as poorly as church buildings. In our zeal to be good stewards, we have become protective of our buildings as if we own them. The facilities God has given us are not for our comfort or for us to point to and derive some false sense of value or satisfaction from. We are to use them.

When our little ones fall on the church's tile floors and skin their knees, we cry out to God and ask for carpeting. Once the carpeting comes, we no longer let the children play on it. We protect it because we need to be good stewards. And after all, where will we get new carpeting if this gets ruined? Frankly, I think we act this way because we have forgotten whose carpeting it is and how we got it in the first place. The new carpeting will probably come from the same place as the old carpeting.

Why not open our facilities for the use of Alcoholics Anonymous or Alcoholics Victorious groups? Support groups for individuals and families need large rooms in which to meet. What about some of those rooms that sit idle in many church buildings all week except for Sunday and Wednesday? How about having a section in the church library or tract rack making available information about these problems that rip apart families? Brochures that describe available church and community resources are very helpful. Since many churches' secretaries are in the building during much of the week, the library could even be left open for people to use.

There is no agency in the world that can affirm people in grace except the church. Hebrews 13:9 says, "Do not be carried about with various and strange doctrines. For it is good that the heart be established by grace, not with foods which have not profited those who have been occupied with them." Whether you eat certain foods or not, whether you use chemicals or not, has no power to profit anyone. What establishes us and has the power to confirm us is God's grace.

The world says, "How much money you make is what matters." When the church says, "How much money you give is what matters," nothing different is being said. Both statements represent "various and strange doctrines." Both focus on deriving worth from human activity, and both statements contradict the Bible. The Bible proclaims God's mercy and grace as the only source of human life and worth. Faith in God is the only means to receive it. Only Christ's performance makes it possible. Every other message from society urges us to try to acquire life, value, and meaning from things we have or do. When these messages result in "good" religious activities, they are hard to confront. When those messages come from Christian families or churches, it is tragedy.

The main purpose of Christian families and the body of Christ is to convince their members of three things:

1. They are loved and accepted based upon the fullness of the one doing the loving and not upon the performance of the one receiving love.
2. They are important, valuable, needed members of the system.
3. They are not alone to live full, meaningful lives in a world that says that life and meaning must be acquired and protected by self-effort.

Churches and families that fulfill this purpose will be places where there is good news for chemically dependent persons and those who love them.

13

Pinning Down the Problem

Have you ever dropped a thermometer while trying to see if you or someone else had a fever? I remember one time as a young boy when my mom decided to take my temperature. Usually it was to prove that, contrary to my urgent pleas, I really was fit to go to school that day. It was a September to May ritual at my house. On this particular occasion, she was right in her assessment, which called for desperate measures on my part. So I removed the thermometer from my mouth and attempted in every way I knew how to make it register enough of a fever to play hooky that day.

I was looking in the mirror practicing my "sick look." At one point I was holding the thermometer in my hands and trying to create sufficient friction to register enough degrees to provide the excuse I needed. Then suddenly it slipped out of my grasp and shattered. As I tried frantically to gather up the shards of glass so I could move them to the bed (where I was supposed to be anyway), I noticed a little drop of mercury pulsating on the dresser. I was fascinated. I became caught up in trying to pin that drop down under my finger. Unfortunately for me, I was so preoccupied with this that I didn't notice my mom watching me from the doorway. Unlike the mercury, which had continued to elude me by scooting off to the side, my illusion and "scooting" was over, and I was on my way to school.

Nevertheless, from that day on I loved playing with mercury, and through my elementary years there would be many broken thermometers to prove it. Imagine how delighted I was still later in high school physics when we were actually allotted mercury to work with. I even managed to do some of the assigned experiments.

This is fine and good for childhood curiosity and classroom experiments. Unfortunately, oftentimes that's what it's like when you are dealing with someone's addiction. I can't tell you how many frustrated family members have used that very phrase, "like trying to put my finger on mercury," as they attempted to describe what it has been like to first understand the addiction of a loved one and then get them the help that was needed.

Finding a Language

What I am really talking about here is the phenomenon of *diagnosis*. The word itself comes from a combination of Greek words that simply mean "to know." The *Merriam-Webster Dictionary* says that diagnosis is "the art of identifying a disease from its signs and symptoms" and "an investigation or analysis of the cause or nature of a condition, situation, or problem."

It is essential to have a "language" to use when trying to understand and then seek help for a problem. For instance, it would be like noticing a change in how you felt but not knowing why. What you *did* know is that you felt generally fatigued. You began to nap more, or take walks, or eat more fruit. But nothing really seemed to help. Then you went to the doctor and were diagnosed as having type 2 diabetes. Once you had the right "language" to describe the problem, you discovered that there were many things you could do, many resources available that would actually help.

I am *not* suggesting that family members become expert diagnosticians when it comes to identifying problems in one another. In fact, I have seen countless cases where, in their need to find the "perfect" diagnosis, they wait too long to take steps to begin a helpful process. In other words, it has been easier to *think* about an addiction than it has been to *do* something about it. I *am* suggesting, however, that it is important to at least have enough of a language to recognize addiction as addiction so the resources that are available can be utilized in order to embark upon a truly helpful course of action.

That is the purpose of this final chapter. I will begin first by speaking in general terms about addiction. These are words, phrases, and descriptions that will help you *to know* (diagnose) whether what you are looking at in a loved one is really addiction or not.

As I have continued in the field of addiction and recovery through the years, I have noticed trends emerge and then dissolve with regard to the popularity of certain drugs and their accompanying addictions. And so I will conclude with some more specific telltale signs to watch for when these particular drugs are involved.

What Are You Looking At?

It is not uncommon for clinicians or diagnosticians to give this simple "test," or a variation of it, in order to help people determine if an addiction is present in their own life or the life of someone they love. Even though forms of it have been around for decades, I am not surprised to find that most people I deal with are still unfamiliar with it. Just one yes should raise an eyebrow. Three or more and there's a good chance you are looking at an addiction. Give it a try and see what you think:

- Is alcohol or drugs used to build up confidence or reduce shyness?
- Has alcohol or drugs been used in an attempt to escape life's responsibilities or the consequences of irresponsibility?
- Has money ever become an issue in any way related to alcohol or drugs?
- Have you ever felt guilt, shame, or remorse after using alcohol or drugs?
- Is alcohol or drugs affecting the quality or dynamics of your relationships at home?
- When going out on a social engagement, is alcohol or drugs a part of the event?
- Has your ambition decreased because of alcohol or drug use?
- Is time being spent on alcohol or drugs (use, preoccupation, planning to use) that was meant to be spent otherwise?
- Have friendships been lost related to alcohol or drug use?
- Has your use of alcohol or drugs or your attitudes about it affected your reputation?
- Has another person ever relayed a concern regarding your alcohol or drug use?
- Is your job or business performance being affected by alcohol or drug use?

- Has a Driving Under the Influence of alcohol or drugs citation occurred?
- Have you ever been admitted to a hospital or been taken to jail as a result of your alcohol or drug use?
- Have you ever used alcohol while taking a prescription medication, the use of which prohibits alcohol use?
- Have you ever failed to recall an event or behavior as a result of your alcohol or drug use?
- Has your efficiency with tasks or your general effectiveness as a person been affected by alcohol or drugs (absences from work, suspensions or expulsions from school, neglect of children or household tasks, etc.)?
- Do you use drugs or drink alone?
- Have you ever sought medical advice for conditions related to alcohol or drugs?
- Do you yourself think you might have a problem with alcohol or drugs?
- Have you had a desire, or unsuccessful efforts, to cut down or control your substance use (i.e., promised yourself or someone else that you would quit in the face of a current negative use-related consequence and then used again)?

Learn These Words and Pay Attention

Dependence is a term that is related to how difficult it is for a person to quit using a certain mood-altering substance. If someone continues to use drugs or alcohol in light of evidence of negative consequences and despite the fact that to continue promises more of the same, there is a high likelihood that the person has become dependent upon that substance (see test above). With physical dependence, the body has adapted to the presence of the drug, and withdrawal symptoms may occur if use is reduced or stopped.

Tolerance describes how much of a substance is needed to quench the increasing desires a user has for a drug or alcohol. There is *physical tolerance* as well as *mood tolerance*. Physical tolerance with alcohol occurs because the liver becomes more efficient at metabolizing it. Simply put, alcohol is sugar and toxins (poison). Hence the word *intoxicated*. When a person is intoxicated (drunk), it just means that they have put more poison in their body and have done it more quickly than their liver can process. In effect, they are poisoned. But as time goes on, the liver becomes more efficient at the task, and so more poison must be added to get the same effect.

When I say mood tolerance, I just mean that it takes a bigger alteration of the mood to get the same satisfaction as before. For example, after a while, it's no fun to bungee jump off a bridge anymore. Now the person must jump off a hot air balloon. This is why someone can lose their family over gambling. There is no substance involved, but there is a mood-altering phenomenon that, for an addict, must be increased to satisfy their desire.

Withdrawal describes the occurrence and seriousness of the symptoms experienced by the user when they are not using their addictive substance. In the case of alcohol withdrawal, symptoms range from mild (shakiness, anxiety, rapid mood swings) to medium (nausea and vomiting, headaches, sweating, insommia) to heavy (convulsions, hallucinations, seizures). A person who experiences heavy withdrawal symptoms is in grave physical danger, potentially a life-threatening state, and needs a medical detoxification to withdraw safely.

In the case of addiction to marijuana (yes, marijuana is addicting), it's not the person's body that signals the absence of the substance, but rather their mood. In other words, when a pot addict is not using, their mood "misses" pot.

To avoid or "treat" their physical withdrawal, a chemically dependent person will use their substance of choice to relieve or avoid withdrawal symptoms. A "mood addict" is less discriminating in their method of withdrawal management and will substitute any number of mood-altering substances. To convince themselves or someone looking on that there is not a problem, a common phenomenon and accompanying rationalization is used by the addict and often accepted by those concerned. They "cut back" to less serious drugs. They stop using hard liquor and just drink beer (please note that there is the same amount of alcohol in a shot of liquor, a glass of wine, and a can of beer). Or they no longer use cocaine and just use pot. In any case, when addiction is present, their efforts to cut back are meaningless. Because mood altering is still taking place, take no comfort in the fact that you or someone you love is switching from one mood-altering substance to another.

Current Trends

These days I spend most of the time in my role as crisis interventionist. For a further understanding of what this means, see my website at www.jeffvanvonderen.com. Not too long ago I was called by a family to do an intervention on a family member whose drug of choice was methamphetamine (crystal meth). This forty-one-year-old male and former university professor was living alone. He had constructed an elaborate water filtering system to remove "the mind control agents the city was adding to the water supply." Several closed-circuit television cameras were strategically placed around the property because he was "in danger of being assassinated by the Mexican mafia." He agreed to meet with the family and me, but insisted on leaving the house and going to the hotel where they were staying. While it was only two miles away, it took him more than thirty minutes to get there because he traveled a circuitous route of side streets to lose the FBI, who "have been trailing him" everywhere he goes. Upon arrival at the hotel he wondered if I had noticed the hot-air balloon with "the surveillance camera that was spying on his movements." Believe me when I say that this was not half of the drug-induced paranoia he exhibited over the course of our meeting.

The use of and addiction to methamphetamine is currently very prevalent, at least as far as I can tell from the frequency of calls I receive to help people with this problem. More on this particular drug in a moment. Government agencies and the private sector spend millions of dollars each year studying and trying to make sense of current trends in the use of alcohol and other drugs. Right now I simply want to tell you what I am noticing. The fact that I mention these particular substances is in no way intended to minimize the seriousness of addiction to the ones I don't mention.

Illicit Drugs

Crack and Cocaine

Cocaine is a powerfully addictive substance. Users sniff or snort it in powder form, inject it in liquid form, and smoke it as well. Free-base use and smoking crack cocaine involves inhaling the fumes produced (called a "clean burn" as opposed to the "dirty burn" produced when smoking pot), usually in some variation of a small glass pipe. "Crack" is the street name used when cocaine is combined with ammonia or baking soda. It makes a crackling sound when heated. Compulsive cocaine use develops rather quickly.

In the nervous system, cocaine interferes with the function of dopamine, which affects the user's physical movements and pleasurable state. Side effects include dilated pupils and increased blood pressure, temperature, and heart rate. A cocaine habit is very expensive. The high from snorting it may last up to thirty minutes, from smoking perhaps up to ten minutes.

Cocaine users exhibit periods of irritability, restlessness, and anxiety. It is not unusual for an addict to fall further into cocaine use to reach the same kind of pleasure as they did from their very first experience. This form of *tolerance* accounts for the person's continued use, despite the cost and other harmful consequences. High doses of cocaine, or use over an extended period of time, can produce a state of paranoia. Crack is known to produce violent and paranoid behavior. Snorting cocaine for a prolonged period can cause ulcers in the nose or even cause the septum to perforate. Depression occurs when cocaine use is curtailed. Cocaine overdose can cause cardiac arrest, seizures, and paralyzation of the person's respiratory system.

There is another danger present when using this substance that is little known, even to many cocaine users. Mixing cocaine and alcohol triggers the liver to combine the two substances and create another substance entirely, called cocaethylene. This multiplies the effects of both substances and increases the chances of sudden death. Cocaine-related emergency room admissions exceed those of heroin, as well as methamphetamine.

Heroin

Heroin use and addiction is probably the country's most publicized of all drug problems. It seems to me that recently there are more people snorting or smoking it. This might be because users think it is safer than needle use, with regard to transmission of the HIV virus. It is not. On the street it is called smack, skag, junk, H, and other "pet" names by users.

Heroin use has serious health implications, some of which are spontaneous abortion, collapsed veins, liver disease, heart and valve infections, overdose, and staph infections (I recently saw a woman who looked like a shark-attack victim from the number of staph infections, operations, and skin grafts resulting from use of dirty needles). Of course, more commonly known problems associated with bad needles are contraction of HIV/AIDS and hepatitis.

An initial surge or rush of pleasure is experienced upon initial use, as well as dry mouth, a heavy sensation in the arms and legs, and a warm sensation on the skin. What is left is a state of alternating periods of alertness and sleepiness. I recently saw this cycle repeat itself several times while on a plane escorting someone to treatment. In this case, the drug that was involved was not heroin but rather morphine (the drug from which it is processed). Withdrawal from the drug produces pain in the bones and muscles, sleep disorder, diarrhea, vomiting, and cold flashes. Sudden withdrawal can sometimes be fatal, although less dangerous than alcohol withdrawal.

Marijuana

I am choosing to address marijuana in this chapter because it is the most commonly used illicit drug in the United States. Street terms for marijuana (and THC-containing substances) include pot, herb, weed, grass, widow, ganja, and hash. Studies estimate that there are approximately 2.6 million new marijuana users every year. It accounts for the third most common drug-related emergency room admissions each year.

Immediate effects of marijuana use include distorted perception of reality, memory and learning impairment, loss of motor skills, impaired problem-solving ability, and increased heart rate. During the first hour after using marijuana, the user's risk of heart attack goes up more than four times. Long-term marijuana use can cause changes in the brain similar to those seen after long-term use of other major drugs of abuse. Marijuana impairs the user's ability to remember and learn information. Not only does this make daily life more difficult, but it makes it more likely that they will trail others in gaining the knowledge and skills necessary to function in school, job, and social settings.

Club Drugs

Club drugs include alcohol, LSD (Acid), MDMA (Ecstasy), GHB, GBL, Ketamine (Special-K), Fentanyl, Rohypnol, amphetamines, and methamphetamine.

Methamphetamine

Methamphetamine is a powerfully addictive drug in the *stimulant* category. It is manufactured in illegal, concealed laboratories from rather inexpensive over-the-counter ingredients; hence it is available for widespread misuse.

Street names of methamphetamine include speed, meth, and chalk. In its smoked form, it is often referred to as ice, crystal, crank, and glass. It is a white, odorless, bitter-tasting crystalline powder. It can be smoked, injected, or ingested. Sometimes the user dissolves the substance in alcohol or water. The effects of methamphetamine can last six to eight hours. After the initial "rush," there is typically a state of high agitation that in some individuals can lead to violent behavior. When crystal is smoked in a glass pipe like crack cocaine, the high can sometimes last more than twelve hours. Even the residue in the pipe can be resmoked.

If you are dealing with someone using methamphetamine, as with most stimulants, you will observe a pattern of bingeing and crashing, where the person can be awake and active (or overactive) for days, then sleep for long periods, even days at a time. Specific effects during awake times are increased physical activity and decreased appetite.

Methamphetamine is extremely addictive and toxic. Large doses can raise the body temperature to dangerous, sometimes fatal levels, as well as cause the user to convulse. Violent behaviors, sleep disturbance (even when not using), confusion, and anxiety can also be present. Use over a long period of time can cause a state of drug-induced psychosis. In this state, the user will be paranoid, hear voices, see things that aren't there, feel things on their skin that aren't there. The extreme paranoia can result in homicidal (to them, self-protective) and suicidal thoughts and behaviors, as well as increasing isolation from interaction and social contexts. Even after use is curtailed, symptoms can last for months, even years.

Ecstasy (MDMA)

Ecstasy is an illegal drug that acts as both a stimulant and hallucinogen, producing an energizing effect, as well as distortions in time and perception and enhanced enjoyment from tactile experiences. Typically, it is taken by mouth, usually in tablet or capsule form, and its effects last approximately three to six hours. It is not uncommon for many tablets of Ecstasy to contain other drugs, which can have their own harmful effects, including methamphetamine, dextromethorphan, cocaine, or ephedrine. In addition, Ecstasy is rarely used alone, most often with pot or alcohol.

Ecstasy is fast-acting and produces feelings of empathy, emotional and mental stimulation, decreased anxiety, heightened well-being, and increased sensory awareness (perception, touch). On the downside, it can produce raised blood pressure, anxiety, cramping, blurred vision, and nausea. In cases of overdose, the user can experience panic attacks, loss of consciousness, seizures, and heart failure. Withdrawal symptoms include irritability, sadness, depression, disinterest in sex, diminished appetite, and in some, aggressive behavior.

Prescription Medication

The most commonly abused prescription drugs that I see fall in the *opioid* (synthetic opiate) category. These medications are commonly prescribed because of their pain-relieving properties. Among the drugs that fall within this class are morphine, codeine, and prescription medications with names like Darvon, Dilaudid, Demerol, and Lomotil, to name a few. Two others are of particular concern in this chapter because of, again, the frequency with which I encounter them in an intervention setting.

These are Oxycodone (OxyContin) and Hydrocodone (Vicodin). Like other opioids, they block the transmission of pain messages to the brain. In addition, they can also affect areas of the brain in which we perceive pleasure. They can also produce drowsiness, cause constipation, make it hard to breathe, and in the case of overdose, paralyze respiration and result in death.

Regular use of these drugs can become physically addicting (the body *needs* the drug), which means that withdrawal symptoms will be experienced when use of the drug is stopped. These can include agitation, cold flashes, muscle and bone pain, sleep disturbance, gastrointestinal problems like vomiting or diarrhea, and muscle twitching.

Over the Counter

Destromethorphan

Destromethorphan is an ingredient commonly found in cold and cough medications. However, when a person consumes many times the recommended dose, they can experience hallucinations and symptoms similar to some of the more serious club drugs. Because the drug impairs the user's vision and cognitive abilities, they are at risk of self-injury while under the influence. Physical symptoms of abuse can include vomiting, numbness in the limbs, high blood pressure, irregular heartbeat, and in severe cases of overdose, brain damage, unconsciousness, seizure, and even death. Obviously, taking this drug in combination with other drugs, even legal over-the-counter medications, can magnify the intensity of the effects, as is common with any drugs when legal or illegal are combined.

If It Looks Like a Duck . . .

. . . and walks like a duck and quacks like a duck, it's probably a duck. While this might seem like an oversimplistic way of seeing things, it tends to work with ducks. And I suggest that it might apply here as well. If it looks like a drug problem and acts like a drug problem and sounds like a drug problem, it's probably a drug problem. If it is, it is a potentially life-threatening situation. And if you wouldn't take half measures with any other life-threatening situation in which you could find a loved one, don't do so with this one either. Pay attention, don't talk yourself out of what you notice, and don't wait. Take aggressive steps to get the help that is needed for all involved.

Additional Resources

For those struggling with addiction-related issues:

Carnes, Patrick. *Out of the Shadows: Understanding Sexual Addiction*. Minneapolis: CompCare Publishers, 1985.

Johnson, Vernon. *I'll Quit Tomorrow*, revised edition. San Francisco: Harper & Row, 1980.

Spickard, Anderson, and Barbara R. Thompson. *Dying for a Drink: What You Should Know About Alcoholism*. Dallas: Word, 1986.

For those struggling with codependency:

Beatty, Meolodie. *Beyond Codependency: And Getting Better All the Time*. San Francisco: Harper & Row, 1989.

———. *Codependent No More: How to Stop Controlling Others and Start Caring for Yourself*. Center City, MN: Hazelden, 1987.

Berry, Carmen R. *When Helping You Is Hurting Me*. San Francisco: Harper & Row, 1989.

For children of alcoholics:

Ackerman, Robert J. *Children of Alcoholics*. Deerfield Beach, FL: Health Communications, Inc., 1988.

Black, Claudia. *My Dad Loves Me, My Dad Has a Disease*. Center City, MN: Hazelden, 1989.

Woititz, Janet. *Adult Children of Alcoholics*. Deerfield Beach, FL: Health Communications, Inc., 1983.

For victims of sexual abuse:

Forward, Susan, and Craig Buck. *Betrayal of Innocence: Incest and Its Devastation*, revised edition. New York: Penguin Books, 1988.

Heitritter, Lynn, and Jeannette Vought, editor. *Helping Victims of Sexual Abuse*. Minneapolis: Bethany House Publishers, 1989.

Peters, David. *A Betrayal of Innocence: What Everyone Should Know About Child Sexual Abuse*. Dallas, Word, 1989.

Wilson, Earl. *A Silence to Be Broken: Hope for Those Caught in the Web of Incest*. Portland: Multnomah, 1986.

For victims of domestic violence:

Miller, Alice. *For Your Own Good: Hidden Cruelty in Child Rearing and the Roots of Violence*, trans., Hildegarde Hannum and Hunter Hannum. New York: Farrar, Straus, and Giroux, 1984.

———. *Thou Shalt Not Be Aware: Society's Betrayal of the Child*. New York: Meridian Books, 1986.

Strom, Kay Marshall. *In the Name of Submission: A Painful Look at Wife Battering*. Portland: Multnomah, 1986.

For those struggling with shame:

Berry, Carmen R. *Loving Yourself as Your Neighbor*. San Francisco: Harper & Row, 1990.

Bradshaw, John. *Healing the Shame That Binds You*. Deerfield Beach, FL: Health Communications, Inc., 1988.

Kaufman, Gershen. *Shame: The Power of Caring*, second edition. Rochester, Vermont: Schenkman Books, Inc., 1985.

Needham, David. *Birthright! Christian, Do You Know Who You Are?* Portland: Multnomah, 1982.

Seamonds, David A. *Healing for Damaged Emotions*. Wheaton: Victor Books, 1980.

———. *Healing Grace*. Wheaton: Victor Books, 1988.

VanVonderen, Jeff. *The Subtle Power of Spiritual Abuse*. Minneapolis: Bethany House Publishers, 1991.

———. *Tired of Trying to Measure Up*. Minneapolis: Bethany House Publishers, 1990.

For those struggling with eating issues:

Antonello, Jean. *How to Become Naturally Thin by Eating More*. Houston: Larksdale, 1988.

Bruch, Hilde. *Conversations With Anorexics*. New York: Basic Books, Inc., 1989.

McFarland, Barbara. *Shame and Body Image: Culture and the Compulsive Eater*. Deerfield Beach, FL: Health Communications, Inc., 1990.

For those wanting "grace-full" parenting skills:

Clarke, Jean I., and Connie Dawson. *Growing Up Again: How to Parent Yourself So You Can Parent Your Children*. San Francisco: Harper & Row, 1989.

Clarke, Jean I. *Self-esteem: A Family Affair*. San Francisco: Harper & Row, 1980.

Miller, Alice. *The Drama of the Gifted Child: The Search for the True Self*. New York: Basic Books, Inc., 1981.

VanVonderen, Jeff. *Families Where Grace Is in Place*. Minneapolis: Bethany House Publishers, 1992.

Recovery Related Tapes by Jeff VanVonderen

Audio

Dealing with People in Despair

Ministry Burnout Is Not God's Idea
Wounded by Shame, Healed by Grace

Audio and Video

Wounded by Shame, Healed by Grace (12-week video plus study
   guide)
Breaking the Silence on Spiritual Abuse
Families Building Healthy People
Good News for the Chemically Dependent

Jeff VanVonderen is an internationally known speaker on addictions and church and family wellness. He has worked as a counselor in both residential and outpatient treatment settings as well as in the religious community, taught at the university level, and is the author of several books, including *Tired of Trying to Measure Up*, *The Subtle Power of Spiritual Abuse*, and *Good News for the Chemically Dependent*. He is one of the featured interventionists on the A&E network's Emmy-winning documentary series *Intervention*, which has also won four Prism Awards. He has also appeared on *Oprah*, the *Today Show*, and *Larry King Live*. He has nine grandchildren and makes his home in Wisconsin.

God Is with You—
No Matter What

Tough times may seem insurmountable, but they are no
match for God! Even when you feel like you can't endure
another day, God is guiding you safely through.

Hope and Help for Hurting Parents

When Your Child Breaks Your *Heart*

Help *for* Hurting Moms

Barbara Johnson

Barbara Johnson tells her family's tragic story and offers hope to families facing similar circumstances. She shares how God brought her through the deep waters without letting her drown—and how he will do the same for us.

Change the way you think . . .
and you can change your life.

Find the inspiration for pursuing your dreams—
right between these pages. You can live a fruitful
and fulfilling life, believing that God will provide
the means to accomplish the impossible.
And the best part is—you can start right now!

Dare to be you and great things will happen!

Success in life is not an accident—but it's not just dumb luck either. If you are ready to achieve positive results in your life, then *Believe You Can!*